Every recipe in this book gives information on:

– **number of servings**
– **preparation time, including cooking time**
– **nutritional value** per portion

The following symbols are used:

  = simple
= more complicated
= demanding

kcal = kilocalories (1 kcal=4.184 kJ)
P = protein
F = fat
C = carbohydrate

NB. 1 gram protein contains about 4 kcal
1 gram fat contains about 9 kcal
1 gram carbohydrate contains about 4 kcal

– If you have a fan-assisted oven, the temperatures given should be reduced by 50°F.

– Times and settings for microwave ovens are only given in the section on microwave recipes.

TASTY APPETIZERS
AND SALADS

RECIPES AND PHOTOGRAPHY

CONSUMER GUIDE AND KITCHEN SKILLS

– Friedrich W. Ehlert –
– Odette Teubner, Kerstin Mosny –

HEARTY HOME COOKING

– Rotraud Degner –
– Pete Eising –

DISHES FROM AROUND THE WORLD

– Rotraud Degner –
– Ulrich Kerth –

RECIPES FOR SPECIAL OCCASIONS

– Marianne Kaltenbach –
– Rolf Feuz –

WHOLEFOOD RECIPES

– Doris Katharina Hessler –
– Ansgar Pudenz –

QUICK AND EASY RECIPES

– Cornelia Adam –
– Michael Brauner –

MICROWAVE RECIPES

– Monika Kellermann –
– Odette Teubner, Kerstin Mosny –

LEAN CUISINE

– Monika Kellermann –
– Volker Goldmann –

Translated by UPS Translations, London
Edited by Josephine Bacon

CLB 4213
Published originally under the title "Das Neue Menu: Vorspeisen und Salate"
by Mosaik Verlag GmbH, Munich
© Mosaik Verlag, Munich
English translation copyright © 1995 by CLB Publishing,
    Godalming, Surrey, UK
Project co-ordinator: Peter Schmoeckel
Editors: Ulla Jacobs, Cornelia Klaeger, Heidrun Schaaf, Dr Renate Zeltner
Layout: Peter Pleischl, Paul Wollweber

Published in the USA 1995 by JG Press
Distributed by World Publications, Inc.
Printed and bound in Singapore
ISBN 1-57215-072-6

The JG Press imprint is a trademark of JG Press, Inc.
455 Somerset Avenue
North Dighton, MA 02764

A FEAST OF GOOD COOKING

TASTY
APPETIZERS
AND SALADS

JG
PRESS

Contents

MAKING ASPIC

BASIC ASPIC RECIPE:

4 ounces potherbs (celery,
*   carrots, turnips, parsley)*
5 ounces lean beef chuck
10 crushed white peppercorns
1 small crushed garlic clove
2 egg whites
1¼ pints beef or chicken
*   broth*
¾ cup wine (white wine,
*   Madeira or sherry)*
1 package powdered gelatin
3 cups cold water
salt

1. Peel and chop the vegetables and place them in a saucepan with the beef, peppercorns, garlic, and egg whites. Add 3–4 tbsps water and stir until well mixed.

2. Add the broth and wine.

3. Bring to the boil, stirring constantly.

4. Cover, and simmer for at least 30 minutes.

5. Add the gelatin to the cold water, stir well and leave until softened.

6. Season the hot broth with salt and strain it through cheesecloth or a coffee filter paper, into the softened gelatin. Stir well, and use as required.

PREPARING A PASTRY CRUST

SHORTCRUST DOUGH:

3½ cups all-purpose flour
¾ cup ice-cold butter or lard
1 tsp salt
1 egg
4–6 tbsps cold water

1. Sift the flour onto a smooth work surface. Grate the butter over it.

2. Add the salt and rub the butter into the flour until the mixture resembles crumbs.
3. Make well in the mixture and break the egg into it.
4. Add the water 1 tbsp at a time, while working out from the center, combining the egg and water with the mixture until it coheres into a dough. Knead just until the dough is smooth.
5. Shape the dough into a ball, wrap it in plastic wrap and refrigerate for 1 hour.

1.

3.

2.

4.

5.

PREPARING A CLASSIC FORCEMEAT WITH FILLING

Hare pâté with hazelnuts en croûte
Use a 1½l/2½ pint pâté mold

FOR THE FORCEMEAT:

1¼ pounds hare(boned)
7 ounces lean boneless pork
8 ounces pork belly
½ tsp freshly ground black
    pepper
1 tsp chopped mixed herbs
6 crushed juniper berries
½ orange
½ lemon

FOR THE FILLING:

1¼ pounds hare fillets
4 slices pickled ox tongue
4 slices cooked ham
salt
ground white pepper
1 tsp clarified butter
1 tsp butter
½ tbsp chopped shallots
6 crushed juniper berries
1 tsp grated orange and
    lemon rind
3 tbsps gin
⅛ cup hare broth
⅔ cup shelled hazelnuts

For the forcemeat:
1. Cut the well-chilled meats into strips.

2. Season with pepper, herbs, and juniper berries.

3. Grate the orange and lemon rinds over the meat.

4. Pass the hare and lean pork twice and the pork belly once through a meat grinder or food processor fitted with a fine disk.

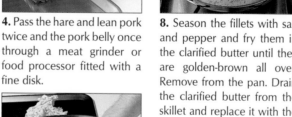

5. In a bowl over crushed ice, add the pork belly to the meat, a little at a time gradually and in small quantities.

6. Press the meat through a round sieve.

For the filling:
7. Trim the hare fillets to fit the mold.

8. Season the fillets with salt and pepper and fry them in the clarified butter until they are golden-brown all over. Remove from the pan. Drain the clarified butter from the skillet and replace it with the butter.

9. Fry the chopped shallots until transparent. Add the juniper berries, grated orange and lemon rind, and then deglaze the pan with the gin, stirring to dislodge any pieces that may have stuck.

10. Pour the broth into the pan. Reduce to a syrup and strain it over the fillets. Cool.

11. Cut the tongue and ham into cubes and work them, together with the hazelnuts, into the prepared forcemeat.

LINING A PÂTÉ MOLD WITH DOUGH

12. Roll out the dough into a rectangle ¼ inch thick.

13. Press the pâté mold over the dough and then use a pastry wheel to cut away the excess dough from around the mold.

14. Dust the sheet of dough with a little flour and fold the sheet over two or three times so that it is as wide as the base of the mold. Place this strip of dough inside the mold and unfold it so that the edges overhang the sides.

15. Shape a small piece of the dough scraps into a ball, dust it with flour and use it to press the pastry against the sides of the mold so that there are no ridges or creases.

16. To ensure that the pastry bakes evenly, press it into the corners of the mold with your thumbs until it is of a uniform thickness.

17. Trim the edges of the pastry to leave a ½-inch overhang.

FILLING THE MOLD

18. Press some of the forcemeat into the mold and ensure there are no air pockets.

19. Place the hare fillets on top of the forcemeat. Pour the meat juices over them and cover with the remaining forcemeat.

20. Place the pâté mold on a damp cloth and press down to ensure that all the air has been forced out.

COVERING THE MOLD

21. Fold the overhanging dough over the forcemeat and brush the strips of dough with a mixture of egg yolk and cream. Cover the forcemeat completely with a thin strip of dough and brush with egg.

22. Place the lid on top and press down well.

23. Use a small metal spatula to press down the edges of the lid.

24. Use the back of a knife to smooth out the pastry surface.

25. Make two openings in the surface. Brush egg around the edge of each opening and add a ring of pastry.

26. Place cylinders of aluminum foil in each opening.

27. Slowly pour the cooled aspic jelly down the holes.

PREPARING TERRINES

Terrines are simply pâtés en croûte without the pastry. They are cooked in a bain-marie and then left to set. The following salmon terrine would make a magnificent appetizer for a celebration meal.

SALMON TERRINE
*For a 1-pint mold
1 cup chanterelles or other
    wild mushrooms
1 tsp butter
salt
ground white pepper
1 tbsp chopped chives
7 ounces fresh salmon
salt
ground white pepper
½ egg white
¾ cup heavy cream, partially
    frozen
8–10 leek leaves
salt*

1. To make the filling, wipe the mushrooms and season them. Sauté them briefly in the butter and reduce the liquid. Set aside to cool.

2. To make the forcemeat, cut the well-chilled salmon into pieces and season with salt and pepper.

3. Grind the fish in a food mixer or chop with a knife. Add the egg white.

4. Slowly add the frozen cream.

5. Press the forcemeat through a drum sieve.

6. Blanch the leek leaves in salted water and then dip them in cold water. Dry carefully on kitchen paper.

7. Lay a sheet of heat-resistant plastic wrap over a template cut to the size of dish. Smooth a thin coating of the salmon forcemeat over the plastic wrap and then cover with the blanched leek leaves.

8. Mix the mushroom filling with the salmon forcemeat and spoon this mixture in a strip onto the leek leaves. (Continued overleaf)

9. Carefully transfer the plastic wrap, leek leaves, and mixture into the mold.

10. Place the mold on a damp kitchen towel and press hard to expel any pockets of air inside. Fit the lid over the mold.

11. Heat the oven to 250°F and cook the terrine in a bainmarie for 30 minutes.

PREPARING A GALANTINE

FOR THE GALANTINE:
1 capon or 1 duck (weighing
   2¾– 3 pounds)
salt
ground white pepper

FOR THE FORCEMEAT:
5½ ounces chicken
4 ounces lean pork
8 ounces fat, salted bacon
salt
ground white pepper
sage

FOR THE FILLING:
4 tbsps pistachio nuts
2 ounces pickled ox tongue
½ cup chicken livers
salt
ground white pepper
4 tsps brandy
4 tsps port

Prepare the forcemeat in the same way as for the pâté en croûte. For the filling, halve the pistachios. Cube the ox tongue. Wash and chop the livers. Mix together, season, and sprinkle with the alcohol. Cover with plastic wrap and marinate for 1 hour in the refrigerator.

1. Remove and discard the wingtips and the feet.

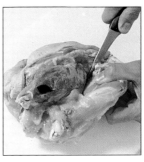

2. Cut down the length of the backbone and loosen the thigh.

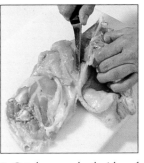

3. Cut down on both sides of the bird through to the breastbone.

4. Pull the ribs and carcass away from the flesh.

5. Cut through the skin and flesh on the wings and remove the bones.

6. Remove the thigh bones and release the drumsticks by pushing the flesh down.

7. Stretch out the boned bird skin-side down.

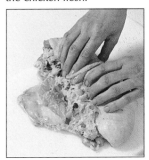

8. Season the inside and spoon the forcemeat across the chicken flesh.

9. Roll up the chicken, with the strip of marinated filling inside, from the rump to the neck.

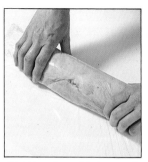

10. Wrap the roll in heat-resistant plastic wrap.

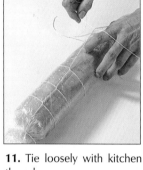

11. Tie loosely with kitchen thread.

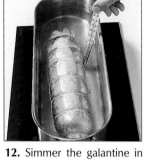

12. Simmer the galantine in broth or salted water at a temperature of 175°F. Allow 45–50 minutes per 2¼ pounds for cooking.

Galantine ready to serve.

PREPARING A MOUSSE

Tomato Mousse
Serves 4–6

*2 ounces tomato flesh, skin
    and seeds discarded*
2 tbsps tomato sauce
1 tbsp tomato juice
1 tbsp tomato paste
cayenne pepper
ground white pepper
pinch of salt
pinch of sugar
1 package unflavored gelatin
1 tbsp broth
⅔ cup whipped cream

1. Press the tomato flesh through a fine sieve and add the tomato sauce, juice, and paste. Season and mix well.

2. Add the powdered gelatin to the hot broth and stir into the tomato mixture.

3. Beat in one third of the whipped cream with a balloon whisk and add the rest a little at a time.

4. Spoon a 1-inch layer of mousse onto a wet tray. Chill.

5. Cut out crescents of mousse and serve with a bay shrimp salad.

Tomato Mousse

MAKING PÂTÉ DE FOIE GRAS

Goose Liver Pâté
For a 1-pint terrine

FOR THE PÂTÉ:
*1½ pounds goose livers
1 tsp chopped mixed herbs
salt
ground white pepper
1 tsp celery salt
3 tbsps brandy
3 tbsps Madeira*

1. Separate the goose livers and carefully remove the membrane.
2. With a sharp knife, slice the goose livers open lengthwise.
3. Carefully remove any blood vessels or tissue.
4. Pull the livers open, exposing the inner surfaces, so that they hold together better when cooking.
5. Sprinkle the herbs, salt, and celery salt over the livers. Place them in a bowl, add the brandy and Madeira, cover, and macerate for 3–4 hours.
6. Line an ovenproof terrine with foil (or thin slices of fat bacon.)
7. Press the marinated livers into the terrine and cover.
8. Heat the oven to 250°F. Place the terrine in a bain-marie and cook for 30 minutes. Leave to chill, and serve sliced.

1.

2.

3.

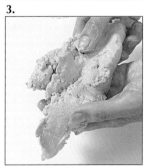

4.

Serve Goose Liver Pâté sliced.

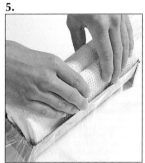

5.

6.

7.

8.

PREPARING A QUINCE SAUCE

*1 cup quince jelly
2 pinches mustard powder
4 tsps apricot brandy
4 tsps white port
1–2 tbsps lemon juice
cayenne pepper
dried apricots and pinenuts
   (pignons)*

1. Press the quince jelly through a fine wooden sieve.

2. Combine the brandy, port, and mustard powder and add to the jelly. Season with lemon juice and cayenne pepper.

3. Slice the apricots into thin strips. Add to the jelly with the pinenuts. Chill and serve with pâtés and galantines.

PREPARING A VINEGAR AND OIL SALAD DRESSING

BASIC RECIPE:
½ garlic clove
1 part vinegar
salt
ground white pepper
sugar
2 parts salad oil
1 tbsp fresh chopped herbs
(parsley, chervil, thyme)

1. Rub the inside of the bowl with the garlic clove. Add the vinegar, salt, pepper, and sugar. Stir until the salt has dissolved.

2. Add the oil a drop at a time. Whisk until the oil and vinegar combine.

3. Add the chopped herbs.

PREPARING A MAYONNAISE-BASED DRESSING

THOUSAND ISLAND DRESSING:
3 tbsps mayonnaise
3 tbsps tomato ketchup
3 drops Tabasco
2 tbsps sour cream or natural yogurt
1 tbsp orange juice
1 tbsp lemon juice
cayenne
salt
1 dried chili, crushed

1. Whisk the mayonnaise, tomato ketchup, Tabasco, and sour cream together.

2. Flavor with the orange and lemon juice, cayenne, and salt.

3. Add the crushed chili.

MAKING HERB VINEGAR AND HERB OIL

Herb vinegar and herb oil should only be made using fresh herbs. Always use a neutral wine vinegar and the best quality salad oil.

Wash the herbs and shake dry in a kitchen towel. To make herb vinegar, use any herb, or use garlic or shallots. To make herb vinegar, combine 7–8 ounces fresh herbs for every quart of wine vinegar. Crush the herbs with a rolling pin, place them in a wide-necked bottle or a preserving jar with a screw-top lid, and add the vinegar. Close the lid tightly and place the jar in the sun for about a fortnight for the flavors to emerge. Strain the vinegar through a coffee filter or cheesecloth and store in a clean jar. Add some fresh herbs to the vinegar to improve the appearance.

It is possible to use a mixture of herbs. If shallots are used to flavor red wine vinegar, then the liquid takes on a quite different aroma. Shallot vinegar is ideal for enriching salad dressings and sauces.

To make herb oil, wash the herbs thoroughly, shake them well and spread them out to dry in an airy, dust-free room. The herbs should not be moist, otherwise the oil will become rancid. Crush the herbs with a rolling pin and place them in a large bottle or jar. Use a good quality salad oil. Seal tightly and leave in a warm, but not hot, place for 3-4 weeks. Strain the oil through cheesecloth into a clean, dry jar and add a fresh sprig of the herb. Store herb vinegar and herb oil in the refrigerator once opened. They will keep for months.

MAKING MAYONNAISE

To make about 1 cup mayonnaise
1 egg yolk, at room temperature
¾ cup salad oil, at room temperature
pinch of salt
pinch of sugar
dash of vinegar
pinch of ground white pepper

1. Beat the egg yolk with a pinch of salt.

2. Add the oil a drop at a time, beating well, then pour it in a thin stream as the mixture emulsifies.

3. Add the seasoning.

*H*ere is your chance to serve up some well-tried favorites but with interesting and exciting variations. Try new methods of preparing those popular appetizers and hors d'œuvres. Parma Truffles or Celery Sticks with Gorgonzola Cream will make a welcome change from the standard soup starter. Add Prunes with Cheese, or Spicy Meat Turnovers to your repertoire of snacks, appetizers, and buffet dishes. Put the nuts and nibbles to one side when friends drop round for a drink. Instead, introduce them to something different. Of all the options available to you on such occasions, there is bound to be something here to tempt you.

Cheese Croissants
(recipe page 34)

PRUNES WITH CHEESE

SERVES 6–8 ■
*Preparation and cooking
time: 10 minutes
Kcal per portion if serving 6:
310
P = 9g, F = 21g, C = 20g*

*30 prunes
6 ounces Swiss cheese
4 slices thinly-sliced,
Canadian bacon, rind
removed*

1. Heat the oven or broiler to 475°F.
2. Soak the prunes in lukewarm water and then make a slit in one side of each prune. Pit them. Cut the cheese into small cubes and stuff them into the prunes. Cut the bacon into strips and wrap a strip around each prune.
3. Bake or broil the prunes for a short time or until the bacon is crisp.
Serving suggestion: serve with fingers of toasted brown bread.

Stuff the cheese cubes into the opened prunes.

Wrap a strip of bacon around each prune and broil.

STUFFED EGGS

SERVES 8 ■
*Preparation and cooking
time: 30 minutes
Kcal per portion (with herb
filling): 145
P = 8g, F = 11g, C = 1g
Kcal per portion (with ham
filling): 135
P = 2g, F = 11g, C = 0.1g*

8 hard-cooked eggs

FOR THE HERB FILLING:
*2 anchovies, soaked in milk
1 tbsp oil
2 tbsps cream
1 tsp horseradish
1 tbsp minced fresh herbs
(cress, dill, chives, chervil)
cress to garnish*

FOR THE HAM FILLING:
*2 slices raw or cooked ham
3 tbsps mayonnaise
½ tsp mustard
salt
generous pinch of paprika
strips of pepper to garnish*

1. Rind and halve the cooled eggs. Remove the egg yolks with a teaspoon. Press them through a sieve.
2. To make the herb filling, chop the anchovies finely. Blend half of the egg yolks with the oil and cream to a smooth consistency. Add the anchovies, horseradish and herbs. Spoon the mixture into a piping bag with a wide nozzle and pipe into the egg white halves. Garnish the stuffed eggs with cress.
3. For the ham filling, chop the ham finely or purée it in a blender. Mix the remaining egg yolks to a smooth cream with the mayonnaise, mustard, and salt. Add the ham purée and season with paprika. Spoon the mixture into a piping bag with a wide nozzle and pipe into the remaining egg white halves. Garnish with strips of pepper.
4. Arrange the stuffed eggs on a bed of lettuce leaves.

Serving suggestion: serve with buttered pumpernickel or granary bread.

> ### TIP
> *Another filling
> suggestion: purée
> 1 tbsp capers and
> 2 tbsps tunafish
> in oil. Blend the
> hard-cooked eggs
> to a smooth
> cream with 2
> tbsps of the oil.
> Add the grated
> rind and juice of
> ½ a lemon, a
> little salt, and the
> tunafish and
> caper mixture.
> Spoon into a
> piping bag with a
> wide nozzle and
> pipe the mixture
> into the egg white
> halves. Garnish
> with capers and
> slices of olive.*

PARMA TRUFFLES

SERVES 6 ■
*Preparation: 20 minutes
Cooling time: 1 hour
Kcal per portion: 515
P = 16g, F = 34g, C = 26g*

*10 ounces pumpernickel
⅔ cup butter
1 cup Parmesan cheese,
freshly grated
3 tbsps whisky
generous pinch of cayenne
pepper
½ cup walnut halves*

1. Crumble the pumpernickel. Cream the butter and add 7 ounces of the pumpernickel, the Parmesan cheese and whisky. Season with cayenne pepper and leave to stand for 10 minutes.

2. Shape the mixture into small balls. Coat the balls with the remaining pumpernickel crumbs and top with a walnut half. Chill the truffles in the refrigerator for 1 hour before serving.

DEEP-FRIED MUSHROOMS

SERVES 4 ■
*Preparation and cooking
time: 25 minutes
Kcal per portion: 215
P = 10g, F = 9g, C = 23g*

*1¼ pounds button
mushrooms
clarified butter or oil for
frying
4 tbsps all-purpose flour
2 eggs, beaten
½ tsp salt
1 cup breadcrumbs
a few parsley sprigs
lemon segments*

1. Carefully wipe the mushrooms but do not wash them. Rinse lightly and dry thoroughly with kitchen paper.
2. Heat clarified butter or oil in a sauté pan or deep-fryer.
3. Add salt to the beaten eggs and dip the mushrooms in the egg mixture and then in the breadcrumbs.
4. Fry the mushrooms until golden-brown. Remove with a slotted spoon and leave to drain on absorbent kitchen paper. Fry the parsley until crispy.
5. Arrange the mushrooms with the parsley and lemon segments on a dish. Serve hot.
Serving suggestion: serve with rémoulade sauce and French bread.

LIVER PÂTÉ

SERVES 10 ■

Preparation time: 3 hours
Cooling time: 12 hours or
overnight
Kcal per portion: 665
P = 15g, F = 63g, C = 1g

1¼ pounds lean shoulder of
pork
8 ounces pigs' or calves' liver
1¼ pounds Canadian bacon
2 onions
1 sprig each parsley,
tarragon, thyme
1 bayleaf
4 tsps cognac
2 eggs
salt
2 tbsps pickled green
peppercorns
a few wide strips of
Canadian bacon for the
dish
1 pork caul

1. Coarsely grind the pork, liver, and bacon. If possible, ask your butcher to do this.
2. Peel the onions and grind them with the herbs and cognac in a food processor. The onion should be well chopped but not reduced to a purée.
3. Place the ground meat, the onion mixture, eggs, and green peppercorns in a large bowl and mix thoroughly. Season generously with salt and 1 tbsp of the liquid from the pickled peppercorns.
4. Preheat oven to 400°F.
5. Line a 2½-pint terrine with bacon. Mold the mixture into a round or oblong meatloaf, depending on the shape of the terrine. Wash the pork caul thoroughly and wrap it round the meatloaf. Place the meatloaf in the terrine, smooth side upward.
6. Cover the terrine with a lid, or seal it tightly with aluminum foil. Place the terrine in a bain-marie, filled with hot water to 1in below the sides of the mold. Place on the lower shelf of the oven and cook for 2½ hours.

Shape the meatloaf and wrap the pork caul around it. If a pork caul is not available, simply cover the surface with bacon.

Place the terrine in a bain-marie filled with hot water.

7. Remove the terrine lid and leave to cool overnight. Cut into slices and serve.
Serving suggestion: serve with gherkins or Cumberland sauce and buttered whole-wheat or whole-grain bread.
Recommended drink: beer or a full-bodied vin de pays.

HAM PÂTÉ IN ASPIC

SERVES 12 ■

Preparation and cooking
time: 2 hours
Cooling time: 12–24 hours
Kcal per portion:
305
P = 17g, F = 20g, C = 1g

1¼ pounds juicy ham cut into
finger-thick slices
8 ounces shoulder of veal
1 cup chicken livers
7 ounces raw, streaky bacon,
rinds removed
3 shallots
a few sprigs parsley
1 egg
¾ cup port
4 tsps cognac
salt
freshly ground black pepper
1 crushed bayleaf
generous pinch each of
ground cloves and ginger
pinch of thyme
butter for greasing
½ cup white wine
¼ bayleaf
1 clove
4 gelatin leaves or 1 tbsp
powdered gelatin

1. Chop 10 ounces cooked ham into cubes and mince the shallots. Grind the remaining ham with the veal, chicken livers, bacon, shallots, and parsley in a food processor. Beat the egg lightly and add to the ground meat together with half the port and the cognac. Mix together thoroughly and season well with salt, pepper, and the herbs and spices. Add the cubed ham.
2. Butter a 3-pint earthenware terrine. Preheat the oven to 400°F.
3. Fill the terrine with the mixture and smooth the surface, pressing down firmly. Cover the dish with aluminum foil and replace the lid, ensuring that it fits tightly.
4. Place the terrine in a rectangular bain-marie, filled with hot water to 1 inch below the sides of the mold. Cook for 1½ hours on the middle shelf of the oven.
5. Leave the terrine to cool, pouring off and reserving any liquid that may have formed. Cover the terrine with a weighted wooden board and leave to cool.
6. Soak the gelatin in just enough water to soften it and degrease the reserved liquid. Add the white wine and the rest of the port and cognac, plus the bayleaf and clove. Boil for 5 minutes and then add the softened gelatin. Strain the liquid through a sieve over the ham pâté.
7. Chill for 12–24 hours in the refrigerator before serving.
Serving suggestion: serve with piccalilli or a sweet pickle.
Recommended wine: a full-bodied burgundy.

TIP

Place a few slices of lemon on the pâté either before or after cooking. These make an attractive garnish if arranged on the meatloaf before adding the aspic. Add some fresh sprigs of rosemary to serve.

CELERY STICKS WITH GORGONZOLA CREAM

SERVES 6 ■
*Preparation and cooking
time: 10 minutes
Kcal per portion: 145
P = 4g, F = 14g, C = 1g*

1 celery heart
4 ounces Gorgonzola cheese
4 tbsps softened butter
½ tsp hot mustard

*Pipe the cheese mixture along the
celery sticks.*

1. Wash the celery sticks thoroughly and discard the leaves. Dry with kitchen paper.
2. Mash the cheese with a fork in a small bowl and add the softened butter and mustard. Mix well.
3. Use a piping bag to pipe the cheese mixture along the celery sticks. Refrigerate until ready to serve.

> **TIP**
>
> *Try using
> Roquefort or
> Stilton instead of
> Gorgonzola.*

BAVARIAN SAUSAGE SALAD

SERVES 4 ■
*Preparation and cooking
time: 20 minutes
Kcal per portion: 570
P = 20g, F = 50g, C = 1g*

8 thick German sausage links
2 onions

FOR THE VINAIGRETTE:
2 tbsps vinegar
salt
1 tsp hot made mustard
4 tbsps oil
freshly ground black pepper
2 tbsps chopped chives for the
garnish

1. Skin the sausages and cut into thin slices. Arrange the slices in overlapping layers in a shallow bowl.
2. Peel the onions, slice them into rings, and spread over the sausage slices.
3. To make the vinaigrette, whisk the vinegar, salt, and mustard in a small bowl until the salt dissolves. Stir in the oil. Pour the vinaigrette over the sausage slices and onion rings. Sprinkle with freshly-ground black pepper and chopped chives. Leave to stand for a few minutes before serving.
Serving suggestion: serve with pretzels.
Recommended drink: cold German beer.

CHEESE CROISSANTS

(photograph page 28/29)

SERVES 6 ■
*Preparation and cooking
time: 50 minutes
Kcal per 2 portions: 510
P = 15g, F = 41g, C = 16g*

1 package (10 ounces) frozen
puff dough
4 slices cooked ham
6 ounces Swiss cheese
1 cup heavy cream
1 egg
salt
freshly grated nutmeg
1 tbsp chopped parsley
1 tsp lemon juice
1 egg yolk for the glaze

*Roll up the pastry triangles from
the base.*

1. Leave the puff dough to thaw for 20 minutes.
2. Chop the ham finely, grate the cheese, and combine with the cream, egg, salt, nutmeg, parsley, and lemon juice.
3. Preheat the oven to 450°F. Rinse a baking sheet with cold water.
4. Roll out the puff dough on a floured board and cut 12 triangles with sides about 4 inches in length. Place 1 tbsp of the filling on each triangle.
5. Roll up each triangle from the base and bend back the ends to make a crescent shape. Place on the baking sheet and brush with egg.
6. Bake the croissants for 20 minutes or until golden.
Recommended drink: pils.

SPICY MEAT TURNOVERS

SERVES 6-8 ■
*Preparation and cooking
time: 50 minutes
Kcal per 2 portions if
serving 6: 425
P = 11g, F = 33g, C = 16g*

1 package (10 ounces) frozen
puff dough
2 ounces smoked, streaky
bacon
1 large onion
1 tbsp butter
1 cup ground steak
salt
cayenne pepper
generous pinch of paprika
2 hard-cooked eggs
12 stuffed olives
4 tbsps raisins
flour for the worktop

1. Leave the puff dough to thaw for 20 minutes.
2. Dice the bacon and onion, and fry it in the butter until transparent. Add the ground steak and fry for a few minutes. Season with the spices.
3. Chop the eggs and olives and add to the meat, together with the raisins. Add 4 tbsps water and warm through.
4. Preheat the oven to 450°F. Rinse the baking sheet in cold water.
5. Roll out the puff dough on a floured board and then use a glass cookie cutter 3 inches in diameter to cut out circles of dough. Spoon a little filling onto each pastry circle, fold it over and press the edges down firmly. Place on the baking sheet.
6. Place the baking sheet on the middle shelf of the oven and bake the turnovers for 20 minutes. Serve warm.
Recommended drink: dry white wine or lager.

MÂCHE WITH SMOKED SALMON

SERVES 4 ■
*Preparation and cooking
time: 15 minutes
Kcal per portion: 305
P = 13g, F = 26g, C = 2g*

*7 ounces mâche
1 small head endive
1 cup fresh store or wild
    mushrooms
2 shallots
7 ounces smoked salmon
    (lox)
2 tbsps walnuts*

FOR THE VINAIGRETTE:
*2 tsps lemon juice
salt
freshly ground white pepper
1 tsp hot mustard
6 tbsps oil (if possible, 2 tbsps
    walnut oil and 4 tbsps
    neutral oil)*

1. Cut off the sandy roots of the mâche but keep each small-leaved plant whole, only separating the larger-leaved plants. Wash the salad greens in lukewarm water, drain in a sieve, or shake carefully in a salad spinner. Separate the endive leaves and cut into pieces.
2. Wipe the mushrooms and cut into strips. Peel and chop the shallots. Cut the salmon slices into wide strips. Coarsely chop the nuts.
3. Reserve half of the salmon. Place all the salad ingredients in a bowl and mix well.
4. To make the vinaigrette, mix the lemon juice with salt and pepper until the salt has dissolved. Use a balloon whisk to blend in first the mustard, then the oil. The latter should be added very gradually to ensure that the dressing is smooth.
5. Pour the vinaigrette over the salad ingredients and mix thoroughly. Arrange the reserved salmon strips over the salad to garnish.

Serving suggestion: serve with crusty bread rolls or cheese-topped rolls.

CRAWFISH AND MOREL PUFFS

SERVES 6 ■ ■
*Preparation and cooking
time: 1 hour 20 minutes
Soaking time for the morels:
    1 hour
Kcal per portion: 500
P = 14g, F = 35g, C = 17g*

*1 tbsp dried morels
36–48 boiled, fresh crawfish
    or shelled crawfish tails
3 tbsps olive oil
1 carrot
2 shallots
1 leek (white part only)
1 stick celery
1 fennel
3 tbsps cognac
¾ cup white wine (preferably
    Chablis)
1¼ cups crème fraîche
1 tbsp butter
salt
freshly ground white pepper
lemon juice
6 vol-au-vent cases*

1. Soak the dried morels in warm water to cover for 1 hour. Rinse thoroughly under running water to ensure that all pieces of grit have been removed from the folds and creases. Halve or quarter the larger morels. Leave to dry on a kitchen towel.
2. Remove the tails from the crawfish, reserving the heads. Break open the underside and remove and discard the dark vein-like intestine. Open up the claws with a hammer or nutcracker and use a long-pronged fork to remove the flesh. Wash the shells and crush them in a blender.
3. Heat the olive oil in a saucepan and lightly fry the crawfish shells and heads for 6–7 minutes. Wash and dice the vegetables and add to

the shells. Continue to cook until all the liquid has evaporated. Add the cognac and flame the crawfish. Add the wine and reduce, stirring frequently. Add the crème fraîche and continue to simmer for 20 minutes or until creamy.
4. Meanwhile, melt the butter in a skillet and add the morels. Season with salt, pepper, and lemon juice. Cook gently for 20 minutes, stirring occasionally with a wooden spoon.
5. Strain the crawfish sauce through a sieve into a saucepan and season with salt and pepper. Bring to the boil again, add the morels, followed by the crawfish tails. Warm through.
6. Warm the vol-au-vent cases in the oven. Fill them with the crawfish sauce and serve.
Recommended drink: a dry, white burgundy, preferably a Chablis.

SPECIAL HERRING SALAD

SERVES 4 ■
*Preparation and cooking
time: 30 minutes
Kcal per portion: 820
P = 23g, F = 69g, C = 20g*

*4 maatjes (pickled) herrings
4 slices cooked veal
1 large pickle
2 small tart apples
2 celery sticks
2 tbsps walnuts
4 medium baked jacket
    potatoes
4 tbsps wine vinegar
salt
freshly ground black pepper
1 cup mayonnaise
    (preferably home-made)
4 tbsps plain yogurt
2 generous pinches ground
    ginger
a few chervil stalks
½ bunch chives*

1. Soak the maatjes herrings. Peel and core the apples. Cut the herrings, veal, pickle, and apples into strips. Chop the celery sticks and the walnuts. Peel and dice the potatoes.
2. Mix the salad ingredients in a bowl and season with the vinegar, a little salt, and the pepper. Leave to stand for a few minutes.
3. Add the yogurt and ground ginger to the mayonnaise. Chop the herbs finely and stir into the salad ingredients together with the mayonnaise. If possible, leave the salad to stand for a further 1–2 hours.
Serving suggestion: serve with crusty bread rolls.
Recommended drink: chilled beer and schnapps or aquavit.

SMOKED FISH SALAD

SERVES 4 ■

Preparation and cooking time: 20 minutes
Marinating time: 1 hour
Kcal per portion: 525
P = 25g, F = 34g, C = 22g

3 smoked fish fillets (smoked whitefish, peppered mackerel, smoked trout)
4 baked jacket potatoes
1 small onion
1 pickle
2 dessert apples
1 red pepper
salt
3 tbsps wine vinegar
3 tbsps chopped dill
½ head chicory to garnish

FOR THE VINAIGRETTE:
2 tbsps wine vinegar
2 tsps hot mustard
salt
freshly ground black pepper
2 tbsps grapeseed oil
6 tbsps cream

1. Cut the smoked fish into pieces, remove the skin and any remaining bones from the other smoked fish and then break them up into smallish pieces.
2. Peel the potatoes and cut into large cubes. Peel and dice the onion and slice the pickle thinly. Peel, core, and quarter the apples and cut into cubes. Remove the seeds and white parts from the pepper and cut into thin strips. Blanch briefly in boiling water.
3. Combine all the ingredients except the fish in a bowl, salt lightly, and pour the vinegar over the mixture. Marinate for 1 hour.
4. To make the vinaigrette, combine the vinegar, mustard, salt and pepper, stirring until the salt has dissolved. Gradually add the oil and cream, whisking constantly.
5. Add the smoked fish and dill to the salad. Pour the vinaigrette over it and stir

Measure out all the appetising ingredients.

Carefully remove the bones from the smoked fish.

Pull the skin from each fish fillet.

gently. Refrigerate for at least 20 minutes. Arrange the salad on a dish with strips of endive.
Serving suggestion: serve with a whole-wheat French stick.

AVOCADO FANS WITH SMOKED SALMON

SERVES 4 ■

Preparation and cooking time: 15 minutes
Kcal per portion: 535
P = 9g, F = 52g, C = 3g

½ cup sour cream
3 tbsps cream
1 tsp Dijon-style mustard
juice of ½ lemon
salt
freshly ground white pepper
½ bunch dill
4 slices smoked salmon (lox)
2 ripe avocados

1. Combine the sour cream, cream, and mustard. Season with lemon juice, salt, and pepper. Wash the dill and snip it into short lengths. Slice the salmon into thin strips. Mix the dill and half the salmon with the cream mixture.
2. Halve and pit the avocados, and peel them carefully.

Slice the avocado halves to make a fan-shape.

Use a sharp knife to make incomplete lengthwise cuts so that the slices hold together at the top.
3. Pull the sliced avocados apart into a fan-shape. Arrange on four plates with a spoonful of the dill cream. Garnish with the remaining salmon strips.
Serving suggestion: serve with garlic bread.

ENDIVE SALAD WITH SHRIMP

SERVES 4 ■

Preparation and cooking time: 15 minutes
Kcal per portion: 175
P = 13g, F = 12g, C = 2g

3 endive heads
2–3 cucumbers pickled in mustard seeds
1 punnet cress
1 cup bay or jumbo shrimp

FOR THE DRESSING:
4 tbsps mayonnaise
3 tbsps cream cheese
3 tbsps milk
1 tbsp vinegar
1 tsp curry powder
salt

1. Separate the leaves of the endives. Wash, pat dry, and cut into strips. Slice the gherkins into thin strips. Place both these in a bowl and combine with the shrimp. Snip off the cress with kitchen scissors, add to the bowl, and stir well.
2. Blend the mayonnaise, cream cheese, milk, vinegar, curry powder, and salt until smooth.
3. Pour the dressing over the salad and stir gently.
Serving suggestion: serve with walnut bread or whole-wheat rolls.

> **TIP**
>
> *Crawfish can be used instead of shrimp, freshly cooked and served warm.*

Dishes from Around the World

*T*he range of international dishes on offer in this chapter is bound to satisfy the most dedicated globetrotter. Prepare some of those memorable restaurant or holiday meals in your own kitchen. How do Chinese Shrimp Sesame Seed Toasts appeal? What about Swedish Smoked Eel on Scrambled Egg? Do Russian Cabbage Piroshki or Tempura, a Japanese favorite, tempt you? Or why not try a little of everything! Invite your friends to a party and give them a cook's tour of the world's kitchens. There's also a wide variety of unusual salads and exotic fruits. But this chapter is not only for the imaginative host or hostess who likes to offer his or her guests something out of the ordinary. It is also for the cook who on occasion feels the need to escape from familiar dishes and embark on a culinary journey to foreign lands and exotic delights.

Sushi
(recipe page 45)

41

SCOTCH EGGS

SERVES 4 ■
*Preparation and cooking
     time: 20 minutes
Kcal per portion: 510
P = 19g, F = 41g, C = 9g*

*4 hard-cooked eggs
10 ounces sausagemeat
1 egg
salt
4 tbsps breadcrumbs
oil or clarified butter for
     deep-frying*

*Leave the hard-cooked eggs to
cool and then wrap them in
sausagemeat.*

1. Peel the cooled eggs. Divide the sausagemeat into four equal portions and press it flat. Place a hard-cooked egg in the center of each and wrap the sausagemeat around the egg.
2. Beat the raw egg with a little salt in a bowl. Dip each sausagemeat ball first in the beaten egg and then in the breadcrumbs.
3. Heat the oil or butter in a skillet or sauté pan. Fry the Scotch egg until it is crispy brown all over. Serve warm or cold.
Serving suggestion: serve with hot mustard and a bread roll.
Recommended drink: beer or a gin and tonic.

PUFF PASTRY SLICES WITH ROQUEFORT CHEESE

Millefeuille au Roquefort

SERVES 4 ■
*Preparation and cooking
     time: 30 minutes
Kcal per portion: 660
P = 13g, F = 54g, C = 25g*

*1 x 10-ounce package of
     frozen puff dough
flour for the worktop
4 ounces Roquefort cheese
½ cup cream cheese
1 tsp armagnac
1 cup whipping cream
salt
freshly ground black pepper
1 tbsp chopped chives*

1. Leave the puff dough to thaw for 20 minutes.
2. Pre-heat the oven to 450°F.
3. Rinse a baking sheet with cold water.
4. Roll out the puff dough to a 9 x 18-inch rectangle and then cut into three smaller rectangles, each 9 x 6 inches. Place on the baking sheet and prick well with a fork.
5. Bake on the middle shelf of the oven for 20 minutes or until golden-brown. Leave to cool on a wire rack.
6. While the puff pastry is baking, prepare the filling. Crumble the Roquefort cheese and stir in the cream cheese and armagnac. Whip the cream until stiff. Reserve a quarter of the mixture for decoration but fold the rest into the cheese mixture. Season and refrigerate for 20 minutes.
7. Coat one of the puff pastry slices with half of the cheese mixture, top with the second slice and then smooth the rest of the cheese mixture over the top. Sprinkle with chives. Take the third pastry slice and cut it into eight strips. Lay the

*First cut one large rectangle of
dough and then divide it into
three smaller rectangular sheets
of equal size.*

*Cut the third sheet into eight
equal strips and place them on
the second layer of cheese
mixture. Use a sharp knife to cut
through the two lower layers.*

strips on top of the chives. Using a sharp knife, cut through the two lower layers to make eight slices. Arrange on a plate.
Recommended drink: dry white wine.

> **TIP**
>
> *Use one large
> sheet of frozen
> puff dough,
> rather than
> several smaller
> ones, or use
> sheets of phyllo
> dough, each
> brushed with
> melted butter.*

CARPACCIO

SERVES 4 ■ ■
*Preparation and cooking
     time: 20 minutes
Partially freezing the fillet
     steak: 30 minutes
Kcal per portion: 320
P = 29g, F = 21g, C = 0g*

*14 ounces tender, well-hung
     beef fillet
4 tbsps olive oil
1 cup button mushrooms
a little lemon juice
4 ounces Parmesan cheese, in
     one piece
salt
freshly ground black pepper*

1. Place the beef fillet in the freezer until it is semi-frozen, about 30 minutes.
2. Use a very sharp knife or a food slicer to cut the meat into slices. Flatten each slice with a steak-hammer until wafer-thin. Arrange on a plate, sprinkle with olive oil and refrigerate for 20 minutes.
3. Meanwhile, carefully wipe the mushrooms and slice thinly. Sprinkle with a little lemon juice.
4. Arrange the meat and mushroom slices on a dish. Shave the thinnest possible slice from the Parmesan cheese using a cheese-slice. Scatter the shavings over the mushrooms and sprinkle with a little salt and pepper.
Serving suggestion: serve with French bread.
Recommended drink: Italian white wine, ideally a Soave Classico.

SMØRREBRØD WITH SMOKED EEL
ON SCRAMBLED EGG

NOUVELLE CUISINE BEAN SALAD

Salade d'haricots verts au foie gras

SERVES 4 ∎
Preparation and cooking time: 30 minutes
Kcal per portion: 205
P = 7g, F = 16g, C = 7g

FOR THE SALAD:
11 ounces beans
½ tsp salt
24 asparagus tips (fresh or canned)
8 lettuce leaves
1–2 black truffles (preferably fresh)
4 slices goose liver paté

FOR THE VINAIGRETTE:
2 tsps lemon juice
salt
freshly ground white pepper
2 tbsps grapeseed oil
2 tbsps extra-virgin olive oil
2 tsps sherry or wine vinegar
2 tsps fresh chopped chervil
2 tsps fresh chopped tarragon

1. Rinse the beans and top-and-tail them. Bring plenty of salted water to the boil and cook the beans for 5–8 minutes, depending on their size. The beans should be cooked *al dente*, like pasta.

> **TIP**
>
> *Fresh truffles are not always available and in any case they are very expensive. The salad can be garnished instead with fresh, wild mushrooms.*

2. Remove the beans with a slotted spoon and plunge them into iced water for a few seconds. Drain in a colander.

3. Prepare fresh asparagus tips in the same way. If you are using canned asparagus, simply drain it.
4. Rinse the lettuce leaves. Wipe the truffles, slice them thinly and place them in a bowl.
5. To make the vinaigrette, combine the lemon juice, salt, and pepper. Add both types of oil to the lemon juice, whisking constantly. Finally, add the vinegar and herbs.
6. Arrange the lettuce leaves on a salad dish. Arrange the beans and asparagus tips next to each other. Add a spoonful of vinaigrette to the sliced truffles. Pour the rest over the salad.
7. Arrange the slices of pâté in the middle of the salad dish and garnish with the truffles. Serve at once.
Recommended drink: champagne.

JEWISH ONION CRACKERS

Pletzels

SERVES 10 ∎
Preparation and cooking time: 20 minutes
Resting time: 1 hour 15 minutes
Kcal per roll: 200
P = 5g, F = 6g, C = 30g

14 ounces flour
2 tsps salt
2 tbsps fresh yeast or 1 package dry yeast
1 cup water
3 tbsps oil
flour for the worktop
butter or margarine for greasing
2 egg yolks
2 large onions
poppyseeds to garnish

1. Mix the flour and salt together in a bowl. Make a well in the center. Place the yeast in the well, add half the water, and some of the flour.

Cut dough circles 2 inches in diameter and about ½ inch thick.

Cover and leave in a warm place to activate the yeast.
2. Stir in the rest of the flour, lukewarm oil, and the remaining water and work to a smooth dough. Keep kneading the dough until it comes away cleanly from the sides of the bowl. Cover and leave in a warm place to rise.
3. Grease a baking sheet. Roll out the dough on a floured worktop to a thickness of ½ inch. Cut rings 2 inches in diameter. Place on the greased baking sheet and brush with the beaten egg yolks.
4. Pre-heat the oven to 400°F.
5. Peel and chop the onions. Press a few onions gently and evenly into each dough circle. Sprinkle with poppyseeds. Cover and leave to rise for a further 15 minutes.
6. Place the cookies on the middle shelf of the oven and bake for about 20 minutes or until golden-brown. Serve warm or cold.
Serving suggestion: serve with pickled herring and a green salad.

AVOCADO AND PARMESAN SALAD

SERVES 4 ∎
Preparation and cooking time: 20 minutes
Kcal per portion: 405
P = 20g, F = 32g, C = 6g

4 ounces mâche
1 apple
½ cup mushrooms
1 ripe avocado
juice of 1 lemon
7-ounce piece fresh Parmesan cheese
bunch of dill

FOR THE DRESSING:
2 tbsps wine vinegar
1 tsp mustard
salt
freshly ground black pepper
2 tbsps olive oil
3 tbsps sour cream

1. Remove any limp or withered leaves from the mâche. Cut off the root ends and wash thoroughly.
2. Peel, quarter, and core the apple. Cut it into strips. Wipe the mushrooms and slice thinly. Halve the avocado, remove the stone, and peel the skin. Cut the avocado flesh into slices. Combine the apple, mushroom, and avocado slices and sprinkle with lemon juice. Break the Parmesan cheese into bite-sized lumps.
3. To make the dressing, combine the vinegar and mustard. Add the salt, pepper, oil, and crème fraîche, whisking well.
4. Arrange the salad ingredients on plates and add dressing to each. Chop the dill with scissors and arrange on top to garnish.
Serving suggestion: rye bread rolls or whole-wheat bread.

Recipes for Special Occasions

It doesn't always have to be goose liver pâté, but who would turn down a terrine which ranks as one of the world's finest examples of haute cuisine? This appetizer features on the grandest of menus, and when served with fresh brioche it really is magnificent.

But connoisseurs are also certain to acclaim such quick and healthy appetizers as Mushroom Crêpes with Herbs or Winter Salad with Endive, Apples, and Duck Breast. These recipes, devised with uncanny flair and imagination, transform otherwise simple salads or quick snacks into a culinary experience. Fresh salad ingredients such as dandelion leaves, spinach, avocado, and Chinese cabbage – combined with jumbo shrimp, quails' eggs, or blue cheese – produce little dishes which are quick to prepare and yet display unsurpassed refinement. It is well worth looking over the following pages and preparing yourself for the pleasures of calf's sweetbreads or breast of duck.

*Fish Cocktail
(recipe page 58)*

PUFF PASTRY SQUARES WITH ASPARAGUS AND GOOSE LIVER PÂTÉ

SERVES 6–8 ■ ■
*Preparation and cooking
    time: 50 minutes
Kcal per portion if serving 6:
    505
P = 9g, F = 39g, C = 26g*

*salt
1 tsp butter
1 tsp sugar
1¼ pounds asparagus
1¼ pounds frozen puff dough
4 ounces goose liver pâté
1 egg white
2 egg yolks
2 tbsps heavy cream*

1. Bring 3 pints of salted water, the butter, and sugar to the boil in a large saucepan. Peel the asparagus and cut off the woody stems. Cook for 15–20 minutes. Leave to cool and then drain. Cut into small pieces.
2. Heat the oven to 450°F.
3. Roll out the puff dough to a thickness of ⅛ inch and make a rectangle 5 inches wide. Cut out 2½-inch squares of dough. Coat each square with a little goose liver pâté, leaving a ½-inch margin at the edges.
4. Place one or two pieces of asparagus on half of the dough squares. Lightly whisk the egg white and brush it over the edges; cover with the remaining halves. Press down firmly.
5. Line a baking sheet with aluminum foil and place the pastry squares on top. Mix the egg yolks with the cream. Make a tiny pattern of dots on top of each square with the tines of a fork and brush with the egg-and-cream mixture.
6. Bake on the middle shelf of the oven for about 15 minutes.

Cut the puff dough into squares.

Coat each square with a little goose liver pâté.

Add one or two pieces of asparagus to half of the squares. Cover with the remaining halves and press the edges together.

Before baking, make a pattern on top of each square with a fork.

ASPARAGUS SALAD WITH CALF'S SWEETBREADS

SERVES 4 ■ ■
*Preparation and cooking
    time: 35 minutes
Soaking time: 2 hours
Kcal per portion: 205
P = 15g, F = 14g, C = 3g*

*8 ounces calf's sweetbreads
1 egg
8 green asparagus spears
4 white asparagus spears
salt
1 tsp sugar
2 tbsps butter
2 cups meat broth
1 onion
½ bayleaf
1 clove
1 tbsp chervil, chopped
1 tsp parsley, chopped*

FOR THE DRESSING:
*1 tbsp red wine vinegar
1 tbsp liquid honey
2 tbsps hazelnut oil
salt
freshly ground white pepper*

1. Place the sweetbreads in cold water and leave to soak for at least 2 hours.
2. Boil the egg for 9 minutes and then plunge into cold water. Peel the asparagus and cut off the woody stem. Bring 1 quart salted water, the sugar, and 1 tsp butter to the boil and add the asparagus. Boil for 15–20 minutes. The asparagus should still be firm.
3. Boil the meat broth in a small saucepan. Peel the onion and stud it with the clove and bayleaf. Place the sweetbreads in the broth with the onion and simmer very gently for 6 minutes. Leave to cool in the broth.
4. Drain the asparagus. Cut off the tips and cut the spears into 1-inch lengths.
5. To make the dressing, combine the wine vinegar, honey, and hazelnut oil. Season with salt and pepper.

Mix the asparagus lengths with two thirds of the vinaigrette. Arrange on four plates and top with the asparagus tips. Pour the remaining vinaigrette over them. Peel the egg and chop finely.
6. Remove the sweetbreads from the broth and discard the membrane and any other impurities. Pat dry with kitchen paper. Cut the sweetbreads into 1–2-inch slices. Heat the rest of the butter. Dip both sides of the sweetbread slices in the melted butter. Serve warm sprinkled with the herbs and chopped egg.
Serving suggestion: crusty mixed-grain bread or rye bread.
Recommended drink: a dry white wine.

STUFFED ARTICHOKES WITH MORELS

SERVES 4 ■ ■ ■
Preparation and cooking
time: 1 hour 20 minutes
Kcal per portion: 530
P = 13g, F = 39g, C = 26g

4 slices cooked ham
¼ cup dried morels
¾ cup chicken broth
5½ ounces frozen puff dough
4 large artichokes
1 lemon
salt
1 egg yolk, beaten with 2 tsps
  water
1 tbsp sesame seeds
  (optional)
7 ounces cream
4 shallots
1 ounce butter
4 tbsps dry sherry
freshly ground white pepper
½ tsp marjoram, chopped
pinch of cayenne pepper

1. Cut the ham into thin strips. Rinse the morels thoroughly in running water. Place them in a bowl and pour on the chicken stock.
2. Heat the oven to 450°F. Thaw the puff pastry.
3. Break off the stems of the artichokes just below the base. Cut off any other leaves so that the artichokes will stand upright. Trim away the tough outer leaves with scissors and remove the top quarter of the leaves with a sharp knife. Rub all the cut surfaces with half a lemon.
4. Bring 5 pints salted water to the boil and add the artichokes with the leaves facing downwards. Cover and cook for 30–35 minutes, the cooking time depending on the size and freshness of the artichoke. They are ready when a leaf can easily be detached. Leave the artichokes to cool in the liquid .
5. Meanwhile, roll out the puff dough until it is ⅛ inch thick. Cut four hearts, stars or other shapes from the

dough. Brush them with beaten egg yolk and place on a rinsed baking sheet. Sprinkle with sesame seeds if liked. Bake on the middle shelf of the oven for 10–15 minutes.
6. Remove the artichoke leaves, the choke and the small, lilac-coloured leaves. Return the hearts to the liquid until you are ready to use them.
7. Take three-quarters of the leaves and scrape away the flesh with the blunt side of a knife. Place the flesh in a blender with the cream and make a purée.
8. Peel the shallots and fry them gently in half the butter. Strain the soaking liquid from the morels through a coffee filter paper and add to the shallots. Boil for 5 minutes. Strain the liquid through a sieve, pressing the shallots with a wooden spoon. Cook the morels in this liquid for 10–15 minutes.

> **TIP**
>
> *Rub lemon juice onto the cut surfaces to prevent discoloration.*

9. Gently fry the strips of ham in the remaining butter. Add the sherry to the morels and reduce the liquid to about 3 tbsps. Add the cream mixture and reduce to a smooth, creamy texture. Add the strips of ham and season with salt, pepper, cayenne pepper and marjoram.
10. Warm the artichoke hearts and the remaining leaves in their liquid. Drain well and place the hearts on warmed plates; stuff them with the morel mixture. Garnish with one or more pastry shapes and the remaining artichoke leaves.

Use scissors or a sharp knife to cut off the top quarter of the artichoke leaves. Immediately rub the cut surface with half a lemon.

Fill the artichoke heart with the morel filling and serve with the pastry shapes and artichoke leaves.

Serving suggestion: serve with crusty bread as an hors d'œuvre, or with rice as a main course or supper dish.
Recommended drink: a good red wine.

FISH COCKTAIL

(photograph page 54/55)

SERVES 4 ■
Preparation and cooking
time: 25 minutes
Kcal per portion: 225
P = 15g, F = 16g, C = 2g

4 ounces garden cress
10 ounces firm white fish
  fillets (monkfish, redfish)
1 tsp olive oil
4 tbsps mayonnaise
  (preferably home-made)
1 tbsp tomato paste
2 tbsps cream cheese
1 tbsp cognac
½ tsp fresh dill tops
salt
freshly ground white pepper
pinch of cayenne pepper

1. Wash the cress and shake it dry.
2. Slice the fish fillets crossways into ½-inch strips. Brush a steamer insert with olive oil and steam the fish for 2–3 minutes.
3. Fill glasses or bowls with the cress, reserving a handful for the garnish.
4. Combine the mayonnaise, tomato purée, cream cheese, cognac and dill. Season with salt, pepper and cayenne pepper.
5. Arrange the strips of fish on the beds of cress, and coat with the sauce. Chop the reserved cress finely and sprinkle it over the top. Chill well before serving.
Serving suggestion: serve with hot buttered toast.
Recommended drink: dry German Franken wine or a white Graves (Bordeaux).

> **TIP**
>
> *Variation: add a little freshly ground green or pink peppercorns and omit the dill.*

MUSHROOM CRÊPES WITH HERBS

SERVES 4 ■■
Preparation and cooking time: 40 minutes
Resting time: 1 hour
Kcal per portion: 275
P = 5g, F = 21g, C = 16g

FOR THE BATTER:
6 tbsps all-purpose flour
1 large egg
½ cup water
2 tbsps butter
salt
freshly ground white pepper
2 pinches grated nutmeg

FOR THE FILLING:
2 cups fresh wild or
  cultivated mushrooms
1 large shallot, chopped
2 tbsps butter
5 tbsps heavy cream
1 tsp oregano, chopped
pinch of thyme, crushed
1 tbsp parsley, finely chopped
salt
freshly ground white pepper
1 tbsp clarified butter

1. To make the crêpe mix, sift the flour into a bowl. Make a well in the center. Beat the egg with 2 tbsps of the water. Pour this into the well and combine. Melt the butter over low heat and add it to the flour-and-egg mixture. Season with salt, pepper, and nutmeg. The mixture should be fairly liquid. If it is too thick, add a little more water. Leave to stand for 1 hour at room temperature.
2. To make the filling, carefully wipe the mushrooms with kitchen paper. Trim the mushroom stalks. If possible do not wash or wet the mushrooms.
3. Peel and fry the shallot in 1 tsp of the butter until transparent. Add 2 tablespoons of the cream and 3 tbsps mushrooms. Purée in a blender.

4. Melt the rest of the butter in a large skillet. Add the mushrooms and fry over high heat for 5–7 minutes, stirring constantly. Add the oregano, thyme, and parsley. Season with salt and pepper and set aside.
5. Heat a quarter of the clarified butter in a small, non-stick skillet or crêpe pan. Add enough mixture to coat the bottom of the pan and fry the crêpe on one side. Flip over and fry the other side until lightly browned. Make four pancakes and reserve them.
6. Add the mushroom purée to the mushrooms. Warm through, but do not boil. Fill the pancakes with the mushroom mixture, fold over and serve at once on hot plates.
Recommended drink: red Bordeaux or Rioja.

> ### TIP
> *The amount of water required for the mixture depends on the type of flour used. If the mixture is fairly liquid, the pancakes will be thinner and lighter.*

STUFFED MUSHROOMS

SERVES 4 ■■
Preparation and cooking time: 55 minutes
Kcal per portion: 235
P = 5g, F = 21g, C = 6g

16 large store mushrooms or
  ceps (porcini)
salt
2 slices Canadian bacon
1tbsp butter
2 tbsp minced parsley
1 tbsp fresh chopped mixed
  herbs (marjoram, thyme,
  rosemary)
2 garlic cloves
2 tbsps white breadcrumbs
1 egg
1 tbsp heavy cream
freshly ground white pepper
butter for greasing
4 tbsps meat broth
1 tbsp olive oil

1. Wipe the mushrooms and wash quickly under running water. Dry with kitchen paper. Carefully remove the mushroom stalks by twisting them away from the cap. Trim the ends and chop the stalks finely. Cut a slice from the rounded top of each mushroom so that each cap can stand upright. Chop these slices and add them to the chopped stalks.
2. Boil 2 quarts of salted water. Add the mushroom caps and return to the boil. Remove the mushrooms with a slotted spoon.
3. Heat the oven to 400°F.
4. Peel and crush the garlic cloves. Heat the butter in a skillet and fry the bacon. Add the chopped mushrooms, all the herbs, and the crushed garlic. Cook gently until all the liquid has evaporated. Stir in the white breadcrumbs.
5. Beat the egg and cream and pour into the mixture. Season with salt and pepper.
6. Coat a shallow, ovenproof dish with butter and add the meat broth. Place the mush-

Carefully twist out the mushroom stalks without damaging the caps.

Spoon the mushroom mixture into the mushroom cups and place in an ovenproof dish.

room caps in the broth. underside uppermost. Spoon the mixture into the mushroom cups and sprinkle with olive oil. Bake on the middle shelf for 20–25 minutes. Cover with aluminum foil for the first 10 minutes, so that the filling does not brown too quickly or dry up. Serve in the dish.
Serving suggestion: serve with steamed spinach and risotto.
Recommended drink: a strong red wine, such as zinfandel.

ASPARAGUS WITH MANGO SAUCE

SERVES 6 ■■■
*Preparation and cooking
time: 45 minutes
Kcal per portion: 140
P = 5g, F = 10g, C = 7g*

*3 pounds green asparagus
1 ripe mango
juice of ½ lemon
salt
freshly ground white pepper
1 tsp butter
pinch of sugar
2 egg yolks
5 ounces cream*

1. Peel the asparagus spears and snip off the woody ends. Peel the mango and cut the fruit away from the stone. Chop well and purée with the lemon juice in a blender.
2. Bring plenty of salted water to the boil and add the butter and sugar. Tie the asparagus spears into bundles with kitchen thread. Cover and cook in the boiling water for 15–20 minutes. The asparagus should remain firm. Reserve the water.
3. Meanwhile whisk the egg yolks, cream and a little salt in a bowl. Place the bowl in a bain-marie and beat until the egg mixture develops a creamy texture. If the sauce is not to be used straight away, place the bowl in cold water.
4. Before serving, stir the mango purée and 2 tbsps of the asparagus cooking water into the sauce. Season with salt and pepper. Re-heat but do not allow to boil.
5. Lift the asparagus out of the liquid and leave to drain thoroughly. Serve on warmed plates with a folded napkin. The sauce should be served separately.
Recommended drink: Riesling, Sylvaner, Johannisberger or a Pouilly-Fuissé.

Peel the mango carefully.

First cut the flesh from the top, bottom and both sides of the mango. Remove the rest of the flesh from the stone and purée with the lemon juice.

To make a creamy sauce, warm the egg yolks, cream and salt in a bain-marie and beat well.

ASPARAGUS CUSTARDS

SERVES 4 ■■■
*Preparation and cooking
time: 60 minutes
Kcal per portion: 435
P = 7g, F = 39g, C = 6g*

*1¼ pounds asparagus
1¾ pints water
¼ ounce butter
1 tsp sugar*

FOR THE CUSTARDS:
*2 eggs
5 ounces cream
¾ ounce butter
salt
freshly ground white pepper
butter for greasing*

FOR THE SAUCE:
*1 tbsp shallots, chopped
1 ounce butter
1 glass Sauternes
5 ounces cream
salt
freshly ground white pepper
pinch of cayenne pepper*

1. Shorten the asparagus spears by about 1 inch. If necessary, peel the asparagus stems.
Boil the water with the butter and sugar. Boil the asparagus with the tips uppermost for 15–20 minutes. Take care not to overcook. Remove the asparagus and reserve the liquid.
2. Cut about a third of the stem end off the asparagus and cut the spears into smaller pieces. Reduce half the asparagus cooking liquid to about 4 tablespoons.
3. Pre-heat the oven to 250°F.
4. To make the custards, whisk the eggs and add the reduced asparagus liquid and all but 2 tbsps of the cream.
Season with salt and pepper. Melt the butter and add to the mixture. Mix in the chopped asparagus and the reserved cream.
5. Grease ramekins, individual soufflé dishes or dariole moulds with butter and spoon in the asparagus custard mixture. Place the custards in a bain-marie filled with warm water at a temperature of about 175°F and cook for 25 minutes.
6. To make the sauce, fry the shallots in half the butter until transparent. Add the wine and reduce by a half. Pass the mixture through a sieve and return to the pan. Add the cream and reduce until the sauce has a light creamy consistency. Cut the rest of the butter into knobs and add it gradually, stirring well after each addition. Season with salt, pepper and cayenne pepper. Warm the asparagus tips in the remaining liquid.
7. Unmold the custards by running a knife around the edge and invert them on to warmed plates. Coat with the sauce and garnish with the asparagus tips.
Serving suggestion: French bread.
Recommended drink: Sauternes or a dry, full-bodied white wine.

> ## TIP
>
> *Instead of adding pieces of asparagus to the custards, purée the asparagus "thirds" with 1 tbsp of the cooking liquid. To test whether the custards are baked, stick a toothpick in the center. If they are ready, it should emerge clean.*

FENNEL TERRINE WITH JUMBO SHRIMP AND COCKTAIL SAUCE

1 TERRINE SERVES 8 ■■■

*Preparation and cooking
time: 45 minutes
Kcal per portion: 190
P = 14g, F = 10g, C = 7g*

*4 ounces fennel, diced
1 cup raw, shelled jumbo
   shrimp, diced
salt
freshly ground white pepper
cayenne pepper
a few fennel leaves, chopped*

FOR THE FILLING:
*1 pound fennel
¾ cup raw, shelled jumbo
   shrimp
1 egg white
⅓ cup semi-frozen heavy
   cream
salt
freshly ground white pepper
cayenne pepper*

FOR THE COCKTAIL SAUCE:
*6 tbsps sour cream
6 tbsps cream cheese
1 tbsp tomato paste
pinch of cayenne pepper
salt
freshly ground white pepper
1 tbsp brandy (optional)*

1. Cook the diced fennel in salted water until firm. Leave to cool.
2. Pre-heat the oven to 250°F.
3. To make the filling, rinse the fennel, cut it into pieces, and cook in a little water until soft. Purée it and leave it to cool. Cut the cold jumbo shrimp into pieces and then grind them in a food processor. First add the egg white to the chopped shrimp, then the cold fennel purée, and finally the partially-frozen cream. Season with salt, pepper, and cayenne pepper and press the mixture through a fine sieve.

4. Drain the diced fennel and pat dry. Season the diced shrimp with salt and pepper and then mix into the filling together with the diced fennel and leaves. Line a long, narrow 1-quart terrine with foil and spoon in the mixture.
5. With the terrine placed on a damp cloth, press the mixture down firmly and cover with a lid. Place the terrine in a bain-marie on the middle shelf of the oven and cook for 30 minutes. Remove from the oven and leave the terrine to cool while still in the bain-marie.
6. To make the cocktail sauce, combine the sour cream, cream cheese, and tomato paste. Season with salt, pepper, and cayenne pepper. Finally, stir in the brandy.
Serving suggestion: French stick or buttered toast.
Recommended drink: white wine.

> ### TIP
> *To make the cocktail sauce less rich in calories, use a low-fat crème fraîche instead of the sour cream and low-fat cottage cheese instead of cream cheese.*

JUMBO SHRIMP WITH THYME AND BUTTER SAUCE

SERVES 4 ■■■
*Preparation and cooking
time: 30 minutes
Kcal per portion: 300
P = 17g, F = 21g, C = 2g*

*12 jumbo shrimp
salt
freshly ground white pepper
2 sprigs thyme
½ tsp butter*

FOR THE SAUCE:
*2 tbsps shallots, finely
   chopped
2 tbsp white wine vinegar
4 tbsps dry white wine
1 tbsp dry vermouth
2 tbsps cream
6 tbsps cold butter, cut into
   pieces
salt
freshly ground white pepper
1 tsp thyme, chopped*

1. Remove the shrimp heads, open out the tails, and loosen the flesh. Leave the ends of the tails attached to the shell. Remove the brown, vein-like intestine with a sharp knife. Sprinkle the shrimp with salt and pepper. Fill a steamer with 1½ inches water, add the sprigs of thyme, and boil the water.
2. To make the sauce, gently cook the shallots with the vinegar and white wine until only 3 tablespoons of liquid remain. Strain into a large saucepan.
3. Add the vermouth to the broth and bring to the boil. Add the cream and warm through. Whisk vigorously over a gentle heat, while gradually adding the knobs of butter. Season with salt and pepper and add the chopped thyme.
4. Brush the steamer insert with butter and lay the prawns in it. Bring the water back to the boil, cover, and steam for 2–3 minutes.

If you first remove the shrimp heads, the shell will detach easily from the flesh.

Slit open the flesh at the head end and use a toothpick or a fork to remove the brown vein-like intestine.

5. Serve the sauce on four warmed plates and add the shrimp.
Serving suggestion: boiled potatoes, rice, or home-baked white bread.
Recommended drink: white wine or champagne.

FISH SALAD WITH SEAWEED

SERVES 4 ■

*Preparation and cooking
   time: 25 minutes
Kcal per portion: 225
P = 15g, F = 16g, C = 2g*

*7 ounces firm fish fillets (cod,
   Pacific red snapper, shark)
4 ounces salmon or salmon
   trout
salt
freshly ground pepper
4 ounces seaweed (available
   from health food stores)
1 tsp cold-pressed olive oil*

FOR THE DRESSING:
*1 tbsp balsamic or good wine
   vinegar
salt
freshly ground white pepper
4 tbsps cold-pressed olive oil
1 tbsp flat-leaved parsley,
   chopped*

FOR THE GARNISH:
*4 tbsps garden cress
12 cherry tomatoes*

1. Cut the fish fillets and salmon into bite-sized pieces and sprinkle both sides with salt and pepper.
2. Add the seaweed to boiling water, cook for 2–3 minutes, drain, and immediately rinse in cold water.
3. Heat the olive oil in a non-stick skillet and gently fry the fish on both sides just until the flesh turns opaque.
4. To make the dressing, stir together the vinegar, salt, pepper, olive oil, and parsley.
5. Rinse the cress and shake it dry.
6. Arrange the fish slices and seaweed on plates, garnish with cress, and pour the dressing over them.
7. Peel each cherry tomato in a spiral like an apple. Shape the peel into small rosettes and decorate each plate with three rosettes.
Serving suggestion: French bread.
Recommended drink: white wine.

TERRINE WITH TROUT AND SALMON MOUSSE

SERVES 8-10 ■ ■

*Preparation and cooking
   time: 30 minutes
Cooling time: 12 hours
Kcal per portion if serving 8:
   235
P = 7g, F = 18g, C = 9g*

*1 package powdered gelatin
3 slices whole-wheat bread
1¾ cups vegetable broth
salt
freshly ground white pepper
3 ounces smoked trout fillet
½ cup butter
3 ounces smoked salmon
   (lox)
butter for greasing*

FOR THE SAUCE:
*½ cup sour cream
2 tbsps chopped fresh herbs
   (basil, chervil, parsley)
salt
freshly ground white pepper*

1. Soften the gelatin in 3 tbsps cold water.
2. Crumble the whole-wheat bread in a food processor.
3. Heat the vegetable broth to boiling point and then remove the saucepan from the heat. Add the gelatin to the broth and stir well until it has dissolved.
4. Add the breadcrumbs and season the mixture with salt and pepper.
5. Cut the trout fillets into pieces and purée them in a blender. Cream the butter and add half to the trout purée. Season with a little salt and pepper.
6. Purée the smoked salmon and mix it with the rest of the butter. Season with salt and pepper.
7. Butter a 1-quart terrine. Line the terrine with alternating layers of the bread mixture, the trout purée, and the salmon purée, ending with the bread mixture.

8. Leave the terrine in the refrigerator to chill for 12 hours.
9. To make the sauce, combine the sour cream and the herbs. Season with salt and pepper.
10. To serve, cut the terrine into ½-inch slices.
Serving suggestion: garnish with salad greens, such as mâche, cress, chicory, and cherry tomatoes.
Recommended drink: dry white wine.

SARDINE TOASTS

SERVES 4 ■ ■

*Preparation and cooking
   time: 35 minutes
Kcal per portion: 305
P = 7g, F = 15g, C = 33g*

*1 large onion, finely chopped
3 tbsps butter
2 large sardines (fresh or
   frozen)
1 tbsp olive oil
1 small red, hot chili pepper
2 tbsps finely chopped
   parsley
2–3 basil leaves
1 tbsp cold-pressed olive oil
salt
pepper
½ French loaf*

FOR THE GARNISH:
*cherry tomatoes
basil or flat-leaved parsley*

1. Soften the butter at room temperature.
2. Wash the sardines and dry them on kitchen paper. Fry in olive oil for 5 minutes on each side. When cool, remove the skins, head, and bones.
3. Heat the oven to 450°F.
4. Chop the chili pepper. Purée the sardine flesh, butter, onion, herbs, olive oil, salt, and pepper in a food processor. Stir in the chopped chili pepper.
5. Cut the French bread into thin slices. Arrange them on a baking sheet and toast on the top shelf of the oven for 5–6 minutes.

6. To make the garnish, wash the cherry tomatoes and herbs. Dry well.
7. Cover the bread slices with a ¼-inch deep coating of sardine mixture and garnish with a cherry tomato and a sprinkling of herbs.
Serving suggestion: serve with cocktail canapés.
Recommended drink: dry white wine, sparkling wine or cocktails.

TIP

*Sardine Toasts can also be prepared with canned sardines, but take care to remove the bones.
Canned tuna fish is an alternative to sardines. To save time, pile the sardine mixture onto cheese crackers or pumpernickel.*

GOOSE LIVER TERRINE WITH BRIOCHE

SERVES 8–10 ■■■

Preparation and cooking time: 1 hour
Cooling time for the terrine 2–3 days
Rising time for the dough: 10–12 hours
Kcal per portion if serving 8: 390
P = 19g, F = 21g, C = 28g

FOR THE TERRINE:
1¾ pounds fresh goose liver
salt
freshly ground white pepper
1 small glass truffle liquor (optional) or 1 tbsp cognac (or armagnac)
2 tbsps sherry

FOR THE BRIOCHE:
2 tbsps fresh yeast
6 tbsps milk
1 tsp sugar
2 cups all-purpose flour
2 eggs
1 tsp salt
½ cup butter
1 egg yolk, beaten with 2 tsps water

1. Chill the goose liver in a damp cloth in the refrigerator for at least 1 hour.
2. Separate the two lobes of the liver by hand and open up each lobe lengthwise. Carefully remove the membrane from around the liver and also the blood vessels, nerves, or any green parts which have come into contact with the gall bladder. Lay the liver in a shallow bowl and sprinkle all over with salt and pepper.
3. Place half the liver in a 1-quart earthenware terrine. Sprinkle with the sherry and the truffle liquor or cognac. Place the other half on top and press down firmly. Smooth the surface and chill the terrine in the refrigerator for at least 10 hours.
4. Fill a roasting pan with 1in water and place on the mid-

Remove the thin membrane from around both lobes of the liver.

Remove any blood vessels and nerves from the liver. Any green parts which have come into contact with the gall-bladder must also be removed as they impart a bitter taste.

Sprinkle truffle liquor and sherry over one half of the liver and then cover with the other half.

After the liver has cooked, invert the terrine lid and press down on the liver to express the fat.

dle shelf of the oven. Heat the oven to 270°F and warm the water to a temperature of between 150–155°F. Use a thermometer to check the water temperature. Place the terrine in the bain-marie and reduce the oven temperature to 175°F. Cook the goose liver for 20 minutes.
5. Remove the terrine from the oven. Invert the lid and press down on the liver so that the fat emerges and covers the liver. Cover the terrine again. When the terrine has cooled down, leave it in the refrigerator (at 34°F) for 2–3 days. The liver is now ready to serve.
6. To make the brioche, crumble the yeast with 2–3 tablespoons of lukewarm milk and sugar. Sift the flour into a large, warm bowl. Make a well in the flour. Whisk together the salt and eggs and add the rest of the milk. Combine all the ingredients with the flour and knead well. Keep folding the dough, pressing down hard on the worktop. Shape the dough into a ball, cover with a damp kitchen towel and leave to rise at room temperature.
7. Knock the dough back. Cut the butter into dice and knead into the dough until smooth and not sticky. Leave the dough for 10–12 hours in a cool place (50–52°F). Knead well again, continuing to fold and press. Place the dough in a buttered brioche mold. Leave to prove for 20 minutes and then brush with the beaten egg yolk. Bake at 450°F for 20–25 minutes.
8. Bring the terrine to the table and cut the liver into ½-inch slices. Serve with the freshly baked brioche. The liver will keep in the refrigerator at 34°F for 4–6 days. Once the terrine has been partly eaten, cover it with aluminum foil.

Serving suggestion: instead of brioche, try buttered toast, perhaps with port wine jelly.
Recommended drink: Sauternes, Barsac or other dry white wine.

TIP

A top-quality goose liver should be a pinkish-beige color. It should also be firm, but not hard.
To store the liver in a refrigerator, cover with a layer of fat. The warm liver should be weighted down, using a board covered with aluminum foil. Place weights, such as heavy cans or a telephone book or two on the board. This should help the fat to ooze out of the liver. If there is insufficient fat to cover the liver, pour a little melted butter into the terrine.

WINTER SALAD WITH ENDIVE, APPLES, AND DUCK BREAST

SERVES 4 ■■
*Preparation and cooking
time: 40 minutes
Kcal per portion: 315
P = 13g, F = 23g, C = 5g*

1 large duck breast (10
  ounces–12 ounces)
salt
freshly ground white pepper
1 tbsp calvados or applejack

FOR THE SALAD:
1 small tart apple
1 tbsp lemon juice
2–3 Belgian endive heads
1 small red onion
3 tbsps walnuts, chopped
salt
freshly ground white pepper

FOR THE DRESSING:
1½ tbsps wine or sherry
  vinegar
salt
freshly ground black pepper
4 tbsps walnut oil
½ garlic clove

Save the pointed endive tips for the garnish. Cut the rest of the leaves into thin strips.

1. Make a number of parallel incisions in the skin side of the duck breast. Rub salt and pepper into the cuts.
2. Heat a heavy skillet. Place the duck breast in the hot pan, skin side downward. Cook the breast in its own fat for 2–3 minutes or until golden-brown. Turn and fry for a further 2–3 minutes. Cover the skillet and cook the breast for a further 10 minutes over a low heat. Remove the breast from the pan and leave to cool on a wire rack, with a tray underneath to catch the drips. Discard the duck fat and deglaze the pan with calvados or applejack.
3. To make the salad, quarter the apple without peeling it and remove the core. Cut the quarters into thin segments and then cut across each segment to make sticks. Place the apple sticks in a bowl and sprinkle with lemon juice.
4. Wipe the endive and set aside 20 pointed tips for the garnish. Cut the remaining leaves into 1-inch lengths. Cut the lengths into narrow strips. Peel the onion, halve it, and slice it into thin rings. Mix all the salad ingredients together in a bowl and season with a little salt and pepper. Stir a little salt and pepper into the vinegar and then add the oil, whisking well. Peel the garlic, crush it, and add to the dressing.
5. Arrange five endive leaves in a star pattern on four large plates. Spoon the salad into the middle and pour the dressing over it. Slice the duck breast diag-onally into thin slices and arrange them between the endive leaves. Pour the calvados-flavored cooking liquid over the duck.
Serving suggestion: buttered whole-wheat, granary, or crusty black rye bread.
Recommended drink: white Bordeaux, such as Graves, Barsac, or a light red wine.

CHINESE CABBAGE SALAD WITH SHRIMP AND SESAME SEEDS

SERVES 4 ■■
*Preparation and cooking
time: 35 minutes
Kcal per portion: 170
P = 7g, F = 14g, C = 2g*

1 small head Chinese
  (Nappa) cabbage
8 mint leaves
2 tbsps garden cress
4 large raw shrimp
1 tsp groundnut oil
ground anise
1 tbsp sesame seeds

FOR THE DRESSING:
1 tbsp soy sauce
1 tbsp chicken broth
1 tbsp sherry vinegar
1 tbsp sherry
4 tbsps peanut oil
1–2 drops sesame oil
a little salt
ground star anise

Open up the underside of the shell and scrape out the flesh.

1. Cut the Chinese cabbage away from the core and discard the leaf ribs. Cut the leaves into ½-inch wide strips. Wash them well and spin dry. Wash the mint leaves and cress and leave to drain.
2. To make the dressing, stir the soy sauce into the chicken broth. Add the vinegar and sherry and finally mix in the oil. Season with a little salt, ground star anise, and sesame oil.
3. Open up the underside of the shrimp shells and carefully remove the flesh, but leave the end of the tail attached to the flesh. Cut a slit in the upper end of the flesh and remove the dark vein-like intestine.
4. Fry the shrimp in peanut oil over a gentle heat until the flesh is milky white. This will take 3–4 minutes, depending on the size. Sprinkle with ground anise.
5. Toast the sesame seeds in a dry skillet over a medium heat.
6. Combine the Chinese cabbage, mint leaves, and half the dressing. Arrange the salad on plates and garnish with the lukewarm shrimp and cress. Sprinkle with sesame seeds.
Serving suggestion: shrimp crackers or fresh bread.
Recommended drink: rosé.

TIP

If using frozen shrimp, allow plenty of time for them to thaw. Instead of shrimp, small, lightly fried pieces of fish or even sliced chicken breast can be used for the garnish.

Wholefood Recipes

*D*ishes that use only natural ingredients do not have to be boring or spartan, as these dainty dishes, amply demonstrate. Fast food chains would do well to look closely at the delicious recipes for blinis and burgers made from buckwheat. The use of basil in the Herb Cheese Mousse with Cherry Tomatoes is a master stroke – this dish is sure to become a wholefood hit! Whether the main ingredients are expensive such as caviar, rock-lobster tails, fillet of beef, and fried quail or everyday, such as potatoes, beans, lentils, Chinese cabbage and mâche, the startling inventiveness of the appetizers and snacks is no less remarkable than the quality of the finished product.

Terrine of White and Green Asparagus (recipe page 80)

CORNMEAL PANCAKES WITH SPINACH, TOMATOES, AND MOZZARELLA

SERVES 4 ■■■
Preparation and cooking time: 1 hour
Kcal per portion: 605
P = 27g, F = 33g, C = 46g

FOR THE MIXTURE:
1 cup yellow cornmeal
salt
1¼ cups milk
3 eggs
corn oil for frying

FOR THE TOPPING:
4 cups young fresh spinach
salt
50 pinenuts (pignons)
3 tbsps butter
1 shallot, chopped
freshly ground white pepper
freshly grated nutmeg
4 tomatoes
7 ounces Mozzarella cheese

1. To make the pancake mix, place the cornmeal and salt in a bowl. Stir the milk and then the eggs, one at a time, into the mixture. Stir until the batter is smooth, then leave it to stand for 15 minutes.
2. Meanwhile, make the topping. Pick over the spinach leaves and wash them thoroughly. Blanch for 1 minute in boiling salted water. Strain well in a colander and squeeze out the water. Toast the pinenuts in a dry skillet.
3. Heat the butter in a skillet and gently fry the chopped shallot. Add the spinach and toasted pinenuts. Season with salt, pepper, and nutmeg.
4. Wash and slice the tomatoes. Slice the Mozzarella cheese.
5. Heat the broiler and line a baking sheet with non-stick baking paper.
6. Heat the corn oil in a small, non-stick skillet or crêpe pan and make eight

The cornmeal pancake mix must be left to stand for about 15 minutes, before making eight evenly-sized pancakes.

Lay four pancakes on a baking sheet, top with the spinach, tomatoes, and cheese and broil for 3–4 minutes.

thin pancakes of roughly the same size.
7. Place four pancakes next to each other on a baking sheet or flat metal sheet, while keeping the rest warm. Top with the spinach mixture, followed by the tomato slices and Mozzarella cheese. Heat under the broiler for 3–4 minutes or until the cheese melts. Repeat with the remaining four pancakes. Serve immediately.
Recommended drink: Dry red wine.

KOHLRABI WITH MUNG BEAN SPROUTS

SERVES 4 ■
Preparation and cooking time: 20 minutes
Marinating time: 30 minutes
Kcal per portion: 310
P = 7g, F = 27g, C = 8g

4 small kohlrabi
2 small carrots
1 cup mung beansprouts

FOR THE DRESSING:
2 egg yolks
salt
freshly ground white pepper
1 tsp mild mustard
juice of 1 lemon
2 tbsps plain live yogurt
6 tbsps sunflower oil

1. Peel the kohlrabi and scrape the carrots. Grate them coarsely. Pick over the mung beansprouts and mix with the grated kohlrabi and carrots.
2. To make the dressing, whisk the egg yolks, salt, pepper, mustard, and lemon juice until creamy. Gradually add the yogurt, then the oil, while continuing to whisk.
3. Pour the dressing over the salad ingredients and mix everything together thoroughly. Leave to stand for 30 minutes. The vegetables can be marinated separately and served in portions.

AVOCADO SPECIAL

SERVES 4 ■■
Preparation and cooking time: 40 minutes
Kcal per portion: 735
P = 5g, F = 75g, C = 4g

4 small ripe avocados
salt
freshly ground white pepper
2 ripe tomatoes
4 tbsps capers

FOR THE VINAIGRETTE:
salt
freshly ground white pepper
2 tbsps wine or sherry vinegar
6 tbsps grapeseed oil
2 shallots, chopped
1 garlic clove, crushed
4 tbsps chervil

1. Peel the avocados, halve, and pit them. Slice two of the avocados thinly and arrange on four plates. Sprinkle with salt and pepper.
2. Stir together the salt, pepper, and vinegar. Add the oil, whisking well. Set aside four chervil sprigs. Chop the remainder and add to the vinaigrette, together with the shallots and garlic. Brush the avocado slices with a third of the vinaigrette.
3. Blanch the tomatoes, skin them, halve, and chop the flesh into cubes. Cut the remaining avocados into cubes and mix with the capers, tomatoes, and the rest of the dressing.
4. Place the avocado mixture in the middle of the plate and garnish with a sprig of chervil.

AVOCADO SALAD WITH PUMPKIN

SERVES 4 ■

*Preparation and cooking
  time: 30 minutes*
Kcal per portion: 745
P = 6g, F = 72g, C = 8g

*1 cup pumpkin, peeled, seeds
  discarded*
12 pickling onions
salt
2 tbsps pinenuts (pignons)
2 ripe avocados
*bunch of watercress or
  garden cress*

FOR THE DRESSING:
2 tbsps crème fraîche
2 tbsps Mascarpone
1 tsp mild Dijon mustard
salt
freshly ground white pepper
½ tsp ground turmeric
3 tbsps sherry vinegar
*4 tsps sake (rice wine)
  or fino sherry*
½ cup olive oil

1. Cube the pumpkin and peel the pickling onions. Blanch both in salted water for about 1 minute. Drain well.
2. Toast the pine kernels in a dry frying pan. Peel the avocados, halve them, remove the stone and cut the flesh into wedges. Snip off the cress or pull the watercress leaves from the stalks.
3. To make the dressing, combine the crème fraîche and Mascarpone. Add the mustard, spices, vinegar and rice wine or sherry. Add the oil, stirring well.
4. Place the salad ingredients in a bowl without the avocados. Pour the dressing over them and stir. Layer the avocado wedges on a plate and arrange the salad alongside them.
Serving suggestion: serve with poppyseed bread rolls spread with chive butter.

CHINESE CABBAGE SALAD WITH MUNG BEANSPROUTS

SERVES 4 ■

*Preparation and cooking
  time: 30 minutes*
Marinating time: 1 hour
Kcal per portion: 325
P = 5g, F = 27g, C = 14g

1 head Chinese cabbage
1 ripe mango
2 tbsps chopped walnuts
¾ cup mung beansprouts
2 tbsps fresh ginger

FOR THE DRESSING:
1 garlic clove
salt
freshly ground black pepper
2 tbsps soy sauce
2 tbsps white wine vinegar
juice of 2 oranges
6 tbsps sesame oil

1. Remove the outer leaves from the Chinese cabbage, halve, and cut out the tough inner stalk. Slice into thin strips.

> **TIP**
>
> *This salad is easily digestible and will be enjoyed by those who do not normally eat raw vegetables. Chinese cabbage is much more digestible than the European varieties of cabbages.*

2. Peel the mango. Cut the flesh from the stone and slice thinly. Toast the walnuts in a dry skillet. Pick over the mung beansprouts, peel the ginger, and grate it. Mix all the salad ingredients together in a bowl.

*Smell the skin of a mango to
judge whether it is ripe.*

*Cut the flesh away from the
mango stone.*

*Toast the walnuts in a cast-iron
skillet.*

3. To make the dressing, chop the garlic and combine with the salt, pepper, soy sauce, vinegar, and freshly-squeezed orange juice. Add the oil, whisking well.
4. Pour the dressing over the salad ingredients, mix thoroughly, and leave to stand for about an hour.
Serving suggestion: serve with whole-wheat or mixed grain bread.

RED CABBAGE SALAD WITH DUCK LIVER

SERVES 4 ■

*Preparation and cooking
time: 30 minutes*
Marinating time: 1 hour
Kcal per portion: 410
P = 19g, F = 31g, C = 10g

½ red cabbage
2 tbsps cranberries
*2 tbsps freshly-grated horse-
  radish*

FOR THE DRESSING:
salt
freshly ground white pepper
1–2 tbsps red wine vinegar
5 tbsps olive oil
2 red onions, chopped

IN ADDITION:
8 small duck livers
salt
freshly ground white pepper
3 tbsps butter

1. Remove the outer leaves from the red cabbage. Quarter it and remove the tough stalk. Cut the quarters into thin shreds. Place the cabbage shreds in a bowl, together with the cranberries and horseradish.
2. To make the dressing, combine the salt, pepper, and vinegar. Add the oil and chopped onions. Pour the dressing over the salad ingredients. Mix well and leave to marinate for 1 hour.
3. Just prior to serving the salad, remove the membranes and fatty tissue from the duck livers and season with salt and pepper. Heat the butter in a skillet and fry the livers over a high heat for 1 minute on each side.
4. Place the salad on four plates and arrange the duck livers alongside.
Recommended drink: a fruity red wine.

BUCKWHEAT BURGERS AND BLINYS

SERVES 4 ■■■
*Preparation and cooking
time: 1 hour
Kcal per portion: 950
P = 24g, F = 54g, C = 83g*

FOR THE BLINIS:
*¾ cup buckwheat flour, sifted
4 tbsps unbleached white
    flour
1 cup light cream
3 eggs
salt*

FOR THE BURGERS:
*2 young carrots
1 shallot
1 cup cooked buckwheat
    (kasha)
4 egg yolks
bunch of chives, finely
    chopped
dry breadcrumbs
salt
freshly ground white pepper*

FOR THE DRESSING:
*1⅓ cups crème fraîche or sour
    cream
1 tsp French mustard
4 tsps cider vinegar
1 tsp liquid honey
salt
freshly ground white pepper
3 tbsps walnut oil
bunch of chives, finely
    chopped*

FOR THE GARNISH:
*1 small oakleaf lettuce
bunch of mâche
2 tomatoes
1 cucumber*

IN ADDITION:
oil for frying

1. To make the blinis, combine the buckwheat flour and white flour. Add the cream, stirring well with a wooden spoon, followed by the eggs one at a time. Add salt and stir well to make a smooth batter. Leave to stand for 30 minutes.
2. To make the burgers, rinse the carrots and peel the shal-
lot, Dice both vegetables. Mix together with the cooked buckwheat and stir in the egg yolks and chives. Add sufficient breadcrumbs to make a workable mixture. Season with salt and pepper and shape into eight small burgers. Heat the oil in a non-stick skillet and fry the buckwheat burgers over a medium heat, allowing 2–3 minutes for each side. Cover and keep warm.
3. To make the sauce, combine the crème fraîche, mustard, vinegar, salt, and pepper. Add the oil, whisking well. Finally, add the chopped chives.

> **TIP**
> *To cook the buckwheat grains, dry-fry with a beaten egg, stirring constantly, then add 1 cup water and simmer, covered, for 15 minutes.*

4. To make the garnish, rinse the lettuces, wash the tomatoes and cucumber, and slice both thinly.
5. Heat the oil in a skillet and fry 12 evenly-sized pancakes over a medium heat.
6. Cover each blini first with some oakleaf lettuce leaves, then a little sauce and then a burger. Follow with a few tomato and cucumber slices, some mâche a little more sauce and another blini.
Recommended drink: A sparkling, dry white wine.

CRACKED WHEAT PATTIES WITH MUSTARD SPROUT SPREAD AND SMOKED SALMON PÂTÉ

SERVES 6 ■■■
*Preparation and cooking
time: 1 hour
Soaking time: 3–4 hours
Kcal per portion: 450
P = 17g, F = 27g, C = 29g*

FOR THE PATTIES:
*1 cup cracked wheat or
    burghul
1 medium carrot
4 sticks celery
salt
2 tbsps chopped shallots
2 tbsps chopped parsley
3 egg yolks
4 tbsps dry breadcrumbs*

**FOR THE MUSTARD
SPROUT SPREAD:**
*½ cup low-fat soft cheese
2 tbsps plain yogurt
2 tbsps French mustard
1 tbsp lemon juice
4 tsps French vermouth
½ cup mustardseed sprouts
salt
freshly ground white pepper*

FOR THE SALMON PÂTÉ:
*7 ounces smoked salmon
    (lox)
juice of 1 small lemon
4 tsps French vermouth
bunch of chives, finely
    chopped
freshly ground white pepper*

IN ADDITION:
*6–8 tbsps oil for frying
mustard seeds to garnish*

1. Soak the cracked wheat or burghul for 3–4 hours or overnight in plenty of water. Cook for 15 minutes in a pressure cooker or 2 hours in a saucepan. Drain well.
2. Rinse the carrot and celery and slice thinly. Blanch for 1 minute in boiling salted water.
3. Combine the cracked wheat or bulghur, shallots,
parsley, and egg yolks. Add sufficient breadcrumbs to make a workable mixture. Season with salt and pepper.
4. To make the mustard sprout spread, combine the cheese and yogurt. Add the mustard, lemon juice, vermouth, and finally the mustard sprouts. Stir well. If necessary, season with a little salt and pepper.
5. To make the salmon pâté, chop the smoked salmon, then grind finely. Add the other ingredients and season with freshly ground pepper.
6. Shape six small patties from the cracked wheat or burghul mixture. Heat the oil in a non-stick skillet and fry over a gentle heat until both sides are lightly browned.
7. Arrange the patties on six plates, add a spoonful of salmon pâté, followed by a spoonful of the mustard sprout spread. Garnish with mustard seeds.
Recommended drink: Dry white wine.

> **TIP**
> *Mustard sprouts are rather hot, so they should be used sparingly. Sprouted at home, they will take 1–2 days to germinate in the summer or 2–3 days in winter. They can also be bought freshly germinated from health food stores.*

HERB CHEESE MOUSSE WITH CHERRY TOMATOES AND BASIL

SERVES 4 ◼
Preparation and cooking time: 20 minutes
Resting time: about 1 hour
Kcal per portion: 440
P = 12g, F = 41g, C = 2g

FOR THE MOUSSE:
4 ounces Gorgonzola cheese
7 ounces Mascarpone
4 tbsps fresh chopped herbs (parsley, chervil, basil)
salt
freshly ground white pepper
pinch of cayenne pepper
⅔ cup whipping cream

FOR THE SALAD:
20 cherry tomatoes
1 shallot, chopped
salt
freshly ground white pepper
1 tsp wine vinegar
2 tbsps olive oil
30–40 basil leaves

1. To make the mousse, blend the Gorgonzola and Mascarpone with herbs and spices. Whip the cream until stiff and fold into the cheese mixture. Chill for about an hour.
2. To make the salad, wash and halve the tomatoes and mix together with the chopped shallot.
3. Combine the salt, pepper, and vinegar, add the oil, pour this over the tomatoes and leave to marinate.
4. Use two wet tablespoons to make oval shapes from the cheese mousse and place them on four plates. Surround with tomatoes and sprinkle with basil leaves.

POTATO AND LENTIL SALAD WITH QUAIL

SERVES 8 ◼ ◼
Preparation and cooking time: 1 hour
Soaking time: a few hours
Kcal per portion: 395
P = 20g, F = 23g, C = 24g

⅔ cup green lentils
12 new, waxy potatoes
bunch of green onions (scallions)
bunch of chives, finely chopped

FOR THE VINAIGRETTE:
salt
freshly ground white pepper
2 tbsps raspberry vinegar
6 tbsps olive oil
2 shallots, chopped

IN ADDITION:
4 dressed quails
salt
freshly ground white pepper
2 tbsps oil for frying
⅔ cup single cream
½ cup chicken broth
½ cup lentil sprouts to garnish

1. Soak the lentils in plenty of cold water for 2 hours. Drain them, discarding the soaking water and cook in fresh, unsalted water in a pressure cooker for 10 minutes.

> ### TIP
> *This delicious salad makes a small meal for 4 people.*

2. Cook the potatoes, unpeeled, in boiling water for 20 minutes.
3. Wash the green onions and chop finely. Combine the spring onions, chives, potatoes, and lentils.
4. To make the vinaigrette, combine the salt, pepper, and vinegar. Stir while adding the oil. Finally, add the chopped shallots. Marinate the salad ingredients in the vinaigrette and keep warm.
5. Remove the bones from the quails. Salt the breasts and thighs. Heat the oil in a skillet and fry the quail flesh over a high heat, allowing 1 minute for each side. Remove, wrap in aluminum foil and keep warm.
6. Deglaze the skillet with the cream and broth. Bring to the boil and reduce.
7. Arrange the salad on plates, top with fried quail, and pour the sauce over it. Sprinkle with lentil sprouts.
Recommended drink:
A dry rosé or a dry white wine.

The flavor of potatoes boiled in their skins is enhanced if a few caraway seeds are added to the water.

LOLLO ROSSO WITH MUSHROOMS AND MINT CREAM

SERVES 4 ◼
Preparation and cooking time: 20 minutes
Kcal per portion: 345
P = 4g, F = 33g, C = 3g

2 small lollo rosso
16 cup mushrooms, brown-capped if possible

FOR THE VINAIGRETTE:
salt
freshly ground white pepper
1–2 tbsps wine vinegar
5 tbsps olive oil

FOR THE MINT CREAM:
1 lemon
⅔ cup sour cream
about 15 finely chopped mint leaves
salt
freshly ground white pepper
2 tbsps whipped cream
mint leaves to garnish

1. Wash the lettuces and dry them in a salad spinner. Wipe the mushrooms. Do not wash them unless really necessary. Slice them thinly.
2. To make the vinaigrette, combine the salt, pepper, and vinegar and add the oil. Marinate the lettuces and mushrooms separately.
3. To make the mint cream, wash the lemon and shave off wafer-thin slices of rind. Chop finely. Halve the fruit and squeeze out the juice. Combine the sour cream, lemon zest, and juice. Add the mint and season well with salt and pepper. Finally, add the whipped cream.
4. Place 1 tbsp of mint cream in the middle of each plate and arrange lollo rosso leaves in a flower pattern around it. Add the mushroom slices and garnish with mint leaves.

TOMATO MOUSSE WITH CRESS SALAD AND QUAILS' EGGS

SERVES 4 ■■
Preparation and cooking
time: 30 minutes
Resting time: about 4 hours
Kcal per portion: 565
P = 13g, F = 51g, C = 7g

2 cups very ripe tomatoes
2 tbsps butter
2 tbsps tomato paste
a few sprigs of tarragon,
   finely chopped
salt
freshly ground white pepper
pinch of sugar
2 tbsps tarragon vinegar
1 package powdered gelatin
1 cup whipping cream

FOR THE SALAD:
12 quails' eggs
12 ounces garden cress
1 tbsp tarragon vinegar
4 tbsps olive oil

1. Wash and quarter the tomatoes. Remove the stalks. Melt the butter in a saucepan and gently fry the tomatoes. Add the tomato paste and the tarragon leaves. Season with salt, pepper, sugar, and vinegar. Bring the mixture to the boil and reduce slightly.
2. Soften the powdered gelatin in 2 tbsps cold water for 15 minutes. Mix the softened gelatin with the tomatoes.
3. Purée the tomato mixture in a blender and strain through a sieve into a bowl. Whip the cream until stiff. As soon as the tomato mixture begins to set, fold in the whipped cream. Chill for 3–4 hours.
4. To make the salad, boil the quails' eggs for 2–3 minutes, plunge into cold water and peel. Snip off the cress and add to a dressing of salt, vinegar, and oil.

5. Arrange the cress salad in a ring on each of the four plates. Use a tablespoon dipped in hot water to cut out an oval of tomato mousse. Place it in the middle of the cress ring. Place

Reduce the quartered tomatoes, herbs, spices, and vinegar.

Purée the herb-and-tomato mixture.

Dissolve the gelatin in the tomato mixture. Just before the jelly sets, fold in the whipped cream.

three quails' eggs in each cress ring.

TERRINE OF WHITE AND GREEN ASPARAGUS

(photograph page 70/71)

SERVES 6 ■■■
Preparation and cooking
time: 45 minutes
Cooling time: about 4 hours
Kcal per portion: 340
P = 7g, F = 33g, C = 2g

6 ounces white asparagus
6 ounces green asparagus
2 cups beef or vegetable broth
salt
sugar
½ cup butter
1 package powdered gelatin
⅔ cup whipping cream

1. Peel the white asparagus and cut off the woody stems. The green asparagus only needs washing. Cut both varieties into pieces and cook separately in 1 cup broth, each with salt, sugar, and 4 tbsps butter added.
2. Soak the gelatin in 2 tbsps cold water to soften.
3. Purée the two types of asparagus separately; add half the gelatin to each purée. Strain the purées through a sieve.
4. Leave the asparagus purées until they start to set. Whip the cream until stiff and fold half into each purée.
5. Spoon the green asparagus purée into a 10-inch long mold. Pour the white purée over it and then use a spoon handle or knife tip to mingle and swirl the two colours into a marbled effect.
6. Chill the terrine for at least 4 hours. Serve in slices.
Serving suggestion: warm asparagus spears and a light vinaigrette.
Recommended drink: a light, neutral white wine.

HERB TERRINE WITH NEW POTATOES

SERVES 4 ■
Preparation and cooking
time: 40 minutes
Cooling time: about 3 hours
Kcal per portion: 290
P = 24g, F = 10g, C = 23g

1 package powdered gelatin
⅔ cup heavy cream
2 cups low-fat cottage cheese
8 radishes
4 ounces young white radish
   (daikon)
bunch of chives
fresh chervil
5–6 borage leaves
bunch of flat-leaved parsley
juice of 1 lemon
salt
freshly ground white pepper
1¼ pounds new potatoes
1 tsp caraway seeds
parsley leaves

1. Soak the gelatin in cold water. Warm the cream and dissolve the gelatin in it.
2. Mix a little cheese with the cream, stir well, and then add to the remaining cheese.
3. Wash and chop the two types of radish. Cut the chives into rings and chop the remaining herbs. Mix them into the cheese mixture and season well with lemon juice, salt, and pepper. Pour the mixture into ramekins or an 8-inch long terrine. Cover with plastic wrap and refrigerate for at least 3 hours to set.
4. Scrub the potatoes well and cook in salted water with a few caraway seeds. Drain the water and allow the potatoes to cool slightly. Invert the terrine onto a dish, cut into slices, and add the potatoes. Serve garnished with parsley leaves.
Serving suggestion: white radish salad in a yogurt dressing.

BEEF CARPACCIO WITH OAKLEAF AND TAMARILLO SALAD

SERVES 4 ■■
*Preparation and cooking
    time: 30 minutes
Kcal per portion: 550
P = 15g, F = 47g, C = 10g*

1 oakleaf lettuce
4 tamarillos

FOR THE VINAIGRETTE:
*salt
freshly ground white pepper
1 tbsp old balsamic vinegar
1–2 tbsp shallot vinegar
8 tbsps olive oil
4 small shallots, chopped
bunch of chives, finely
    chopped*

IN ADDITION:
*7 ounces partially frozen
    fillet of beef
6 tbsps toasted flaked
    almonds*

1. Remove the oakleaf lettuce leaves, tear into small pieces, and wash well. Dry in a salad spinner. Skin the tamarillos and cut into slices.
2. To make the vinaigrette, stir together the salt, pepper, and both types of vinegar until all the salt has dissolved. Add the oil, whisking well. Dress the oakleaf salad with 2 tablespoons of the vinaigrette dressing. Mix the chopped shallots and chives with the rest of the dressing.
3. Cut the beef into wafer-thin slices. Place the slices inside a freezer bag and flatten with the smooth side of a steak hammer. Arrange the slices on four plates and sprinkle with the dressing.
4. Add the oakleaf lettuce, interleave with slices of tamarillo, and sprinkle with flaked almonds.

Place the beef fillet slices inside a freezer bag and flatten with a steak hammer.

TIP

Tamarillos or tree-tomatoes originate from New Zealand. They are rather tart in flavor and can be eaten raw in salads or cooked as a stewed fruit. Always skin them. Balsamic vinegar comes from northern Italy and is available at good delicatessens. If you cannot find it, use the best quality red wine vinegar.

SAUERKRAUT SALAD WITH SMOKED DUCK BREAST

SERVES 4 ■■
*Preparation and cooking
    time: 40 minutes
Kcal per portion: 730
P = 29g, F = 59g, C = 12g*

2 tart apples
1¾ cups sauerkraut, rinsed
1 small lettuce
2 smoked duck breasts
apple wedges to garnish

FOR THE DRESSING:
*1 cup sour cream
⅔ cup grapeseed oil
3 tbsps wine or sherry
    vinegar
3 tbsps dry sparkling white
    wine
salt
freshly ground white pepper
2 small shallots, chopped
bunch of chives, chopped*

1. To make the dressing, whisk together the sour cream, oil, vinegar, and wine. Season with salt and pepper. Finally mix in the shallots and chives.
2. Chop the sauerkraut. Quarter and core the apples. Grate the flesh finely and mix with the sauerkraut. Marinate in half the dressing.
3. Clean the lettuce. Leaving the inner leaves intact, tear the outer leaves into smaller pieces. Wash and dry in a salad spinner. Cut the duck breasts into thin slices.
4. Marinate the lettuce leaves in the remaining dressing and arrange on four plates. Spoon the apple and sauerkraut onto the leaves and garnish with the duck breast slices and apple wedges.
Recommended drink: white wine.

WATERCRESS WITH KOHLRABI AND APPLE

SERVES 4 ■■
*Preparation and cooking
    time: 40 minutes
Kcal per portion: 300
P = 5g, F = 25g, C = 12g*

2 young kohlrabi with leaves
2 small tart apples
2 bunches watercress
4 tbsps raw peanuts

FOR THE VINAIGRETTE:
*salt
freshly ground black pepper
2 tbsps cider vinegar
5 tbsps groundnut oil
1 small shallot, chopped*

**FOR THE YOGURT
DRESSING:**
*⅔ cup plain yogurt
½ tsp French mustard
juice of 1 lemon
salt
freshly ground black pepper*

1. Wash the kohlrabi. Chop the inner leaves and set them aside for the dressing. Peel the kohlrabi. First cut into slices and then into thin strips. Peel the apples and grate them coarsely. Wash the watercress and dry in a salad spinner. Use the smaller leaves in the salad, reserving the larger ones for the yogurt dressing. Rub the thin skins from the peanuts and split them into halves.
2. Combine the salt, pepper, vinegar, and oil. Add the chopped shallot and the kohlrabi leaves. Marinate the salad ingredients in this dressing.
3. To make the yogurt dressing, purée the larger watercress leaves with the dressing ingredients in a blender.
4. Serve a little cress yogurt on four plates, arrange the salad loosely over it and top with another spoonful of yogurt. Sprinkle with the peanuts.

Quick-and-easy Recipes

This section is a compendium of quick, easy, and delicious appetizers, salads, and snacks. Whether cold, warm, or hot, they will take only a matter of minutes to prepare, need no special culinary skills, and are ideal for single people or busy professionals who expect something a little more appetizing than an omelet or cold meat. The emphasis here is on small but delicious dishes and tempting savories such as Herb Tomatoes au Gratin. Standard fast food fare – hamburgers, pizza, and French fries – will soon take a back seat, in favor of Parma Ham Carpaccio with Mushrooms or Mozzarella and Tomato Toasts. These are just two examples of recipes which are filling and tasty, yet amazingly quick and simple to prepare. Serving suggestions are offered, and many of these appetizers and snacks can easily be converted into entrées.

Green Asparagus with Chervil Cream
(recipe page 89)

83

POTATO AND MUSHROOM SPANISH TORTILLA

SERVES 4   ■■

*Preparation and cooking
    time: 30 minutes
Kcal per portion if serving 2:
    710
P = 22g, F = 54g, C = 28g*

14 ounces Idaho potatoes
8 tbsps olive oil
1 large onion, finely chopped
bunch of chives, chopped
1 cup mushrooms
salt
freshly ground black pepper
freshly grated nutmeg
5 eggs
chives to garnish

1. Wash and peel the potatoes.
2. Heat half the oil in a 9-inch
skillet. Slice the potatoes
thinly and add them to the
pan.
3. Add the chopped onion
and fry for 1 minute, stirring
well.

> ### TIP
> *Give this dish a
> slightly different
> texture by adding
> 4 slices chopped
> ham. Served with
> a tomato salad,
> it makes a
> delightful supper
> for two.*

4. Wipe the mushrooms,
rinse quickly, and dry with
kitchen paper. Slice thinly,
add to the potatoes, and
leave to cook for a little
longer. Add the chives and
season well with salt, pepper, and nutmeg. Remove
from the heat and leave to
cool.
5. Beat the eggs in a bowl
and add the potato-and-
mushroom mixture.

*Using a slicer, slice the raw
potatoes into the skillet.*

*Use a plate to flip the tortilla over
and cook it for a further 10
minutes.*

6. Heat the remaining olive
oil in the skillet and fry the
mixture for about 10 min-
utes. Use a plate to flip the
tortilla over. Cook for a further 10 minutes.
7. Slide the tortilla onto a
plate, sprinkle with chives,
cut into portions, and serve.
Recommended drink: a dry
sherry (fino).

SHRIMP SPREAD ON TOAST

SERVES 4   ■

*Preparation and cooking
    time: 20 minutes
Kcal per portion: 340
P = 10g, F = 18g, C = 33g*

1 cup bay shrimp
⅓ cup cream cheese
salt
freshly ground white pepper
generous pinch of cayenne
    pepper
1 tbsp lemon juice
large bunch of dill
1 small French stick
4 tbsps butter

1. Set aside 12 of the best
shrimp.
2. Mix the remaining shrimp
with the cream cheese and
purée in a food processor.
Season well with salt, pepper, cayenne pepper, and
lemon juice. Chop most of
the dill, reserving a few
sprigs for decoration, and
add it to the mixture. Leave
to chill in the refrigerator.
3. Cut the French stick into
12 slices, each about ¾ inch
thick, and toast the slices.
4. Butter the bread and
spread it with the shrimp
spread. Top with a tiny sprig
of dill and a shrimp. Arrange
on a dish or four plates and
serve.
Recommended drink: a
sparkling white wine.

> ### TIP
> *Another way to
> serve shrimp
> spread is on 2-
> inch sticks of
> celery.*

DRESSED MOZZARELLA ON A BED OF RADICCHIO

SERVES 4   ■

*Preparation and cooking
    time: 20 minutes
Kcal per portion: 335
P = 16g, F = 27g, C = 2g*

2 x 6-ounce packages
    Mozzarella cheese

FOR THE DRESSING:
1 tbsp pink peppercorns
2 garlic cloves
4 tbsps white wine vinegar
6 tbsps extra virgin olive oil
1 tsp fresh thyme leaves
1 tsp fresh oregano leaves

IN ADDITION:
½ cucumber
1 small radicchio

1. Cut the Mozzarella into ¼-
inch cubes.
2. To make the dressing,
crush the pink peppercorns
coarsely, using a pestle and
mortar. Peel and crush the
garlic cloves. Combine the
peppercorns, garlic, white
wine vinegar, olive oil,
thyme, and oregano. Pour
the dressing over the
Mozzarella cubes and leave
for 10 minutes. Stir gently
from time to time.
3. Peel the cucumber and
remove the seed-filled core.
Cut the flesh into cubes the
same size as the cheese and
add to the mixture.
4. Wash the radicchio and
pat it dry. Arrange the larger
outer leaves on four plates.
Cut the smaller leaves into
strips, combine with the
cheese mixture, season
again if necessary, and
spoon over the lettuce
leaves.
Serving suggestion: whole-
wheat bread.
Recommended drink: beer.

ZUCCHINI OMELET WITH SUNFLOWER SEEDS

SERVES 4 ■ ■
*Preparation and cooking
time: 30 minutes
Kcal per portion: 240
P = 10g, F = 19g, C = 4g*

*14 ounces small zucchini
4 tbsps olive oil
2 tbsps sunflower seeds
2 garlic cloves
1 large onion, finely chopped
salt
freshly ground black pepper
4 eggs*

1. Wash and trim the zucchini. Slice thinly or grate coarsely with a grater.
2. Heat the olive oil in a large skillet. Quickly fry the sunflower seeds. Peel and crush the garlic cloves and add to the skillet, together with the chopped onion and grated or sliced zucchini. Cook for 7–8 minutes, stirring frequently. Season with salt and pepper and leave to cool.

Lightly fry the zucchini, garlic, onion, and sunflower seeds.

Add the zucchini mixture to the beaten eggs.

5. Slide the omelet onto a plate and cut into four or eight segments. Serve hot, warm, or cold.
Serving suggestion: serve with fresh bread.
Recommended drink: a light, dry white wine, ideally a Verdicchio.

> **TIP**
> *Replace sunflower seeds with about ½ cup diced salami. Served with a crisp green salad, this makes an excellent supper for two.*

3. Whisk the eggs in a bowl and add the zucchini.
4. Heat the remaining olive oil in the skillet and add the egg and zucchini mixture. Cook over a gentle heat and leave the eggs to set, shaking the pan occasionally to prevent the omelet from sticking. Flip the omelet over with the help of a plate and cook for a further 5 minutes.

MOZZARELLA AND TOMATO TOASTS

SERVES 4 ■
*Preparation and cooking
time: 20 minutes
Kcal per portion: 230
P = 13g, F = 13g, C = 13g*

*2 large beefsteak tomatoes
2 packs Mozzarella cheese
(about 6 ounces each)
4 slices thick-cut whole-wheat
bread
2 tbsps garlic butter
salt
freshly ground black pepper
1 tsp oregano, dried
½ bunch basil to garnish*

1. Wash the tomatoes and remove the stalks. Slice them crosswise into slices ¼ inch thick.
2. Cut the Mozzarella into slices of the same thickness.
3. Toast the bread, and butter it.
4. Heat the oven to 475°F.
5. Alternate layers of Mozzarella and tomato on the bread. Season with salt, pepper, and oregano. Bake for 10 minutes or until the cheese begins to melt. Garnish with basil leaves.
Recommended drink: Prosecco or Orvieto.

> **TIP**
> *Try slices of salami instead of Mozzarella and sprinkle with shredded Jack or Swiss cheese.*

PARMA HAM CARPACCIO WITH MUSHROOMS

SERVES 4 ■
*Preparation and cooking
time: 15 minutes
Kcal per portion: 405
P = 17g, F = 35g, C = 1g*

*10 slices Parma ham, thinly
sliced
¾ cup mushrooms
juice of ½ lemon
salt
freshly ground black pepper
4 tbsps olive oil, extra virgin
leaves from 2 sprigs basil
2-ounce piece Parmesan
cheese*

1. Arrange the Parma ham on four plates.
2. Wipe the mushrooms, rinse quickly, and dry with kitchen paper. Slice very thinly and sprinkle with lemon juice, salt, and pepper.

> **TIP**
> *Try fillet of beef instead of Parma ham. Place the beef in the freezer for at least 30 minutes and then use a very sharp knife or a meat slicer to cut into thin slices.*

3. Arrange the mushrooms on top of the ham and drizzle olive oil over them both.
4. Cut the basil leaves into strips and sprinkle over the mushrooms, followed by the grated Parmesan cheese.
Serving suggestion: serve with crusty white bread.
Recommended drink: a light white wine.

BACON-WRAPPED DATES
WITH PEPPER SAUCE

BACON-WRAPPED DATES WITH PEPPER SAUCE

SERVES 4 ■

*Preparation and cooking
time: 30 minutes*
Kcal per portion: 565
P = 2g, F = 35g, C = 56g

1 large red pepper
3 tbsps olive oil
1 onion, finely chopped
1 tsp sweet paprika
pinch of cayenne pepper
2 tbsps tomato paste
salt
freshly ground black pepper
15 slices smoked streaky
    bacon
24 fresh dates
24 cocktail sticks

1. Halve the pepper and remove the seeds and core. Cut each half lengthwise again and then cut across to make narrow strips.
2. Heat the olive oil in a saucepan and gently fry the strips of pepper and the onion for about 5 minutes. Add the cayenne pepper and paprika and continue to cook. Add the tomato paste, season with salt and pepper, and add ½ cup water. Cover and simmer for 15 minutes.

TIP

*Instead of dates,
try dried apricots
or figs. To reduce
the calories, use
slices of lean
ham in place of
bacon, and
reduce the frying
time accordingly.*

---

3. Meanwhile, cut the rind off the bacon slices and slice them in half. Pit the dates and wrap half a bacon rasher around each one. Secure

Slit open each date with a sharp knife and pit it.

Wrap half a bacon rasher round each date and secure with a cocktail stick.

the bacon with a cocktail stick. Heat a non-stick skillet and fry the bacon for 8–10 minutes or until crispy, turning from time to time.
4. Season the pepper sauce again and pour into a bowl, either as it is or puréed in a food processor.
5. Arrange the bacon and dates in a bowl or on a bed of fresh lettuce leaves. Serve with the pepper sauce.
Serving suggestion: serve with mixed grain bread or a French stick.
Recommended drink: beer or chianti.

HERB TOMATOES AU GRATIN

(photograph page 19)

SERVES 4 ■

*Preparation and cooking
time: 30 minutes*
Kcal per portion: 170
P = 4g, F = 10g, C = 15g

4 large beefsteak tomatoes
4 garlic cloves
2 bunches parsley, finely
    chopped
4 tbsps breadcrumbs
1 egg yolk
3 tbsps olive oil, extra virgin
salt
freshly ground black pepper
1 tsp each thyme and
    oregano, fresh or dried

1. Wash the tomatoes and slice them in half crosswise.
2. Pre-heat the oven to 450°F.
3. Peel and crush the garlic cloves. Place in a bowl and add the parsley and bread-crumbs. Stir in the egg yolk and olive oil and mix well, adding a little more oil if necessary to make the mixture stick together. Season well with salt, pepper, thyme, and oregano. Spoon an equal quantity of the mixture into each tomato half.
4. Place the tomato halves in a soufflé dish and brown in the oven for 15–20 minutes.
Serving suggestion: serve with French bread.
Recommended drink: a light red wine, preferably Italian or French.

GREEN ASPARAGUS WITH CHERVIL CREAM

(photograph page 82/83)

SERVES 4 ■ ■

*Preparation and cooking
time: 30 minutes*
Kcal per portion: 200
P = 5g, F = 17g, C = 5g

1¾ pounds green asparagus
salt
1 tsp butter
pinch of sugar
4 ounces chervil
5 tbsps soya oil
2 egg yolks
juice of ½ lemon
freshly ground white pepper
generous pinch of cayenne
    pepper
freshly grated nutmeg
8 cherry tomatoes

1. Peel the lower third of the asparagus spears and cut off the woody stems. Bring plenty of salted water to the boil with the sugar and butter. Simmer rather than boil the asparagus for 15–20 minutes. The spears should be firm when cooked.
2. Rinse the chervil and snip off the stalks. Set aside a few sprigs, and add the rest to the soya oil, egg yolks, and lemon juice and purée in a blender to make a sauce. Season with salt, pepper, cayenne pepper, and nutmeg.
3. Strain the asparagus in a colander and arrange on four plates. Pour a ribbon of chervil sauce over the asparagus spears. Garnish with the reserved chervil sprigs and the cherry tomatoes.
Serving suggestion: serve with small, new potatoes or toast.
Recommended drink: a light, dry white wine, such as Orvieto or Riesling.

FRIED OYSTER MUSHROOMS WITH TOMATO VINAIGRETTE

SERVES 4
*Preparation and cooking
time: 30 minutes*
Kcal per portion: 220
P = 5g, F = 20g, C = 3g

2 beefsteak tomatoes
3 tbsps red wine vinegar
salt
freshly ground black pepper
8 tbsps olive oil
a few basil leaves
1¾ pounds oyster mushrooms
4–5 garlic cloves

1. Blanch the beefsteak tomatoes, skin and seed them, and chop the flesh.
2. To make the vinaigrette, stir together the red wine vinegar and salt until the salt has dissolved. Add the pepper and half of the olive oil, whisking well until the dressing has a creamy texture. Add the chopped tomatoes. Cut the basil into thin strips and add to the dressing.
3. Remove the tough stalks from the oyster mushrooms, rinse, pat dry, and cut into smaller pieces if necessary.
4. Heat the remaining olive oil in a large skillet and fry the oyster mushrooms well on both sides, pressing them down with a spoon. Peel and crush the garlic cloves and add to the mushrooms. Season with salt and pepper.
5. Serve the oyster mushrooms with a few spoonfuls of the dressing.
Serving suggestion: French bread
Recommended drink: a light red wine, such as Beaujolais Villages.

Blanch and skin the tomatoes.

Scoop out the seeds but leave the connecting flesh.

Chop the tomatoes.

Fry both sides of the oyster mushrooms well.

KIDNEY BEANS WITH FETA CHEESE

SERVES 4
*Preparation and cooking
time: 15 minutes*
Kcal per portion: 615
P = 37g, F = 22g, C = 70g

*16-ounce can red kidney
beans*

FOR THE DRESSING:
*3 tbsps balsamic vinegar or
red wine vinegar*
salt
freshly ground black pepper
4 tbsps olive oil
3 garlic cloves

IN ADDITION:
4 large lettuce leaves
8 ounces Feta cheese
*2 tsps fresh or 1 tsp dried
oregano*

1. Tip the kidney beans into a sieve, rinse well in cold water, and leave to drain.
2. To make the dressing, first peel and crush the garlic cloves. Mix with the vinegar, salt, pepper, and olive oil. Combine the dressing and beans and mix well.
3. Wash the lettuce leaves, pat dry, and arrange on four plates. Spoon the beans over the lettuce leaves.
4. Cut the Feta cheese into four and use your fingers to crumble each slice over the portions of beans. Season with black pepper and sprinkle with oregano.
Serving suggestion: serve with crusty whole-wheat or rye bread.
Recommended drink: full-bodied red wine.

SMOKED PORK MOUSSE WITH SPINACH SALAD

SERVES 4
*Preparation and cooking
time: 25 minutes*
Kcal per portion: 305
P = 15g, F = 24g, C = 1g

*7 ounces boneless smoked
pork*
2 tbsps cream
*½ cup cream cheese with
herbs*
salt
freshly ground white pepper
freshly grated nutmeg
*generous pinch of cayenne
pepper*
2–3 tbsps dry sherry (fino)
2 green onions (scallions)
1 cup leaf spinach
2 tbsps sherry vinegar
3 tbsps oil

1. Chop the smoked pork coarsely and purée in a food processor with the cream.
2. Add the cream cheese, season with salt, pepper, nutmeg, and paprika and mix together well. Add enough sherry to make a smooth creamy texture. Season well and chill in the refrigerator.
3. Trim the green onions and cut the green parts into very narrow rings. Add to the purée and return to the refrigerator.
4. Wash the spinach leaves well and cut off stalks.
5. Make a dressing by combining the rest of the sherry vinegar, salt, pepper, and oil. Cut the white parts of the green onions into rings and dip them and the spinach leaves in the dressing.
6. Arrange the mousse on four plates. Decorate with the spinach and green onion rings.
Serving suggestion: serve with rye bread.
Recommended drink: a young white wine.

FRISÉE WITH GARLIC SHRIMP

SERVES 4 ■
*Preparation and cooking
    time: 20 minutes
Kcal per portion: 195
P = 5g, F = 18g, C = 3g*

*1 small frisée (curly endive)
2 shallots, finely chopped*

FOR THE DRESSING:
*juice of 1½ lemons
1 tsp hot mustard
salt
freshly ground white pepper
7 tbsps soya oil*

IN ADDITION:
*bunch of lemon balm
4–5 garlic cloves
1 cup shrimp*

1. Remove the outer leaves of the frisée and tear the larger leaves into smaller pieces. Wash the leaves and then spin dry. Place the leaves in a bowl, together with the chopped shallots.

TIP

Try 1 cup cooked, chopped ham instead of shrimp.

2. To make the dressing, mix together the lemon juice, mustard, salt, and pepper. Add half the soya oil a few drops at a time, whisking vigorously until the dressing develops a creamy consistency.
3. Pour the dressing over the lettuce leaves. Add half the lemon balm leaves and mix well. Arrange on four plates.
4. Heat the remaining oil in a skillet. Peel and crush the garlic cloves and fry until lightly browned. Add the shrimp and fry over a medium heat for a further 6–7 minutes.

Mix the frisée and shallots together in a bowl.

Add the soya oil to the dressing, whisking constantly until it develops a creamy consistency.

Sprinkle chopped lemon balm over the fried shrimp.

5. Chop the remaining lemon balm leaves finely and stir into the fried shrimp. Serve on the bed of frisée.
Serving suggestion: buttered toast.
Recommended drink: a dry white wine, such as a Riesling.

AVOCADO SALAD WITH EGG SAUCE

SERVES 4 ■
*Preparation and cooking
    time: 25 minutes
Kcal per portion: 400
P = 5g, F = 39g, C = 3g*

*2 eggs
2 ripe avocados
juice of 1 lemon
1 tsp hot mustard
2 tbsps white wine vinegar
salt
freshly ground white pepper
generous pinch of cayenne
    pepper
4 tbsps safflower oil
1 bunch cress*

1. Boil the eggs for 10 minutes, plunge straight into cold water, shell, and leave to cool.
2. Meanwhile, carefully peel the avocados, halve lengthwise and remove the stone with the tip of a knife. Sprinkle immediately with lemon juice to prevent discoloration.
3. Slice the eggs in half lengthwise and carefully remove the yolks. Mash the yolks with a fork and add the mustard, white wine vinegar, salt, pepper, cayenne pepper, and safflower oil. Stir well.
4. Chop the egg whites and add to the mixture.
5. Rinse the cress in cold water. Use kitchen scissors to snip off the sprouts over the mixture. Mix well.
6. Cut the avocado halves into thin slices and arrange on four plates. Top with 1 or 2 tbsps of the egg sauce.
Serving suggestion: serve with buttered toast.
Recommended drink: sparkling wine or champagne.

ALMOND MEATBALLS WITH TWO SAUCES

SERVES 4 ■ ■
*Preparation and cooking
    time: 30 minutes
Kcal per portion: 655
P = 30g, F = 52g, C = 7g*

*½ day-old bread roll
10 ounces mixed ground
    meats
2 tbsps ground almonds
1 egg
1 egg yolk
bunch of parsley, chopped
salt
freshly ground black pepper
1 tsp fresh oregano leaves
pinch of cumin
3 tbsps olive oil
⅔ cup Gorgonzola
2 tbsps Madeira
⅔ cup black olives, pitted
1 garlic clove
juice of ½ lemon*

1. Soak the bread roll in water.
2. Squeeze the water out of the bread. Combine the ground meat, almonds, egg, egg yolk, bread, and half the parsley.
3. Season with salt, pepper, oregano, and cumin.
4. Heat the oil in a skillet. Shape walnut-sized meatballs and fry for 6–8 minutes. Shake the pan well from time to time to ensure the balls are fried evenly.
5. Crush the Gorgonzola with a fork, add the Madeira, and season with pepper.
6. Purée the olives, garlic, and lemon juice in a food processor. Season with salt and pepper and add the remaining parsley.
7. Arrange the meatballs with a little of each of the sauces on four plates.
Serving suggestion: a French stick.
Recommended drink: a dry sherry (fino.)

MÂCHE WITH PASTRAMI AND PARMESAN

SERVES 4
Preparation and cooking time: 20 minutes
Kcal per portion: 265
P = 16g, F = 21g, C = 1g

6 ounces mâche
4 thin slices pastrami

FOR THE DRESSING:
3 tbsps white wine vinegar
salt
freshly ground black pepper
5 tbsps walnut oil
2 shallots, finely chopped

IN ADDITION:
1 tbsp sesame seeds
2-ounce piece Parmesan cheese

1. Trim the mâche and rinse well, as grains of sand and grit often get trapped between the leaves. Dry well in a salad spinner.
2. Slice the pastrami into thin strips.
3. Combine the white wine vinegar, salt, and pepper. Add the walnut oil a few drops at a time, whisking constantly until the dressing develops a creamy consistency. Add the chopped shallots.
4. Toast the sesame seeds in a dry, nonstick skillet until they are lightly browned. Add to the dressing. Toss the mâche and pastrami in the dressing.
5. Arrange the lettuce on four plates. Use a shredder to cut the Parmesan cheese into shreds.
Serving suggestion: serve with toasted, buttered mixed grain bread.
Recommended drink: dry cider.

A crisp, freshly washed mâche.

A TRIO OF VEGETABLES WITH CURRY SAUCE

SERVES 4
Preparation and cooking time: 30 minutes
Kcal per portion: 190
P = 9g, F = 12g, C = 10g

1 kohlrabi
1 baby red beet
bunch of baby radishes with leaves

FOR THE CURRY SAUCE:
1 shallot, finely chopped
1 cup cream cheese
juice of ½ lemon
2 tbsps safflower oil
2 tbsps curry powder
1 tsp honey
salt
freshly ground white pepper
4 tbsps alfalfa sprouts

1. Peel the kohlrabi and the beet. Grate both vegetables using the medium section of a rotary grater.
2. Wash the baby radishes and leaves. Cut a few of the better leaves into thin strips. With a vegetable slicer, slice the radishes very thinly or else cut them by hand. Mix with the radish leaves.
3. To make the curry sauce, combine the chopped shallots, cream cheese, lemon juice, and safflower oil. Add the curry powder and honey. Season with salt and pepper. If the sauce is a little

Cut the radish leaves and add them to the grated or sliced radishes.

too thick, dilute with more lemon juice. Mix half the alfalfa sprouts into the curry sauce.
4. Arrange the grated kohlrabi, beet, and radishes in three piles on each plate. Spoon the curry sauce into the middle and sprinkle with the remaining alfalfa sprouts.
Serving suggestion: serve with whole-grain bread and butter or new potatoes in their skins.

> **TIP**
>
> *Instead of pastrami you could use wafer-thin slices of the best prosciutto or Parma ham. The Trio of Vegetables with Curry Sauce can be varied to suit what is available or in season.*

MUSHROOM SALAD WITH HERBS

SERVES 4
Preparation and cooking time: 25 minutes
Kcal per portion: 145
P = 3g, F = 13g, C = 4g

1 medium carrot
2 lemons, juice squeezed
1½ cups mushrooms
1 tsp horseradish sauce
salt
freshly ground white pepper
generous pinch of cayenne pepper
5 tbsps walnut oil
bunch each of parsley, dill and chives, minced

1. Peel the carrot and grate it coarsely. Sprinkle with a little lemon juice so that the carrot retains its color.
2. Rinse the mushrooms or wipe with moist kitchen paper. Trim the tips of the stalks. Slice thinly – an egg slicer will do the job very rapidly. Sprinkle with a little lemon juice.
3. Combine the rest of the lemon juice and the horseradish sauce. Season with salt, pepper, and cayenne pepper. Add the walnut oil and chopped herbs, and stir well.
4. Gently stir in the mushrooms and grated carrot, and arrange on four plates.
Serving suggestion: serve with rye bread or black bread.
Recommended drink: a light, dry white wine.

Microwave Recipes

*P*eople who know how to use the microwave oven properly will want to use it for the preparation of snacks, appetizers, and salads. There are so many ingredients which will cook beautifully in just a few minutes and combine with salad vegetables to make something really special, such as Braised Calf's Sweetbreads with Salad Greens, or Fillet of Rabbit with Wild Mushroom Salad.

In a microwave oven, dishes such as Cauliflower Pâté with Shrimp or Puff Pastry Rolls Stuffed with Exotic Vegetables need only a minute or two to cook and so retain their natural flavors.

Microwave owners are used to cooking with a minimum of utensils. You will need a few, small, round microwave-safe dishes which should be arranged in a circle in the center the oven. Finally, don't forget to allow all microwaved dishes to rest for 2–3 minutes, as the cooking process continues even after microwaving has stopped.

*Beet Salad with Herb Vinaigrette
(recipe page 100)*

FILLET OF RABBIT

FILLET OF RABBIT WITH WILD MUSHROOM SALAD

SERVES 4 ◼

*For standard microwave
ovens (600 watts)
Preparation and cooking
time: 35 minutes
Kcal per portion: 265
P = 15g, F = 20g, C = 2g*

1 cup chanterelle mushrooms
½ cup ceps (porcini)
1 cup brown-capped store
mushrooms
2 tbsps chopped shallots
1 garlic clove, chopped
6 tbsps oil
salt
freshly ground black pepper
1 tsp thyme leaves
1 tbsp white wine vinegar
1 tsp balsamic or red wine
vinegar
2 boned rabbit fillets (about
8 ounces)
1 tbsp minced parsley

*Season the cooked mushrooms
with the two types of vinegar.*

*Sprinkle salt and pepper over the
rabbit fillets, arrange them in a
microwave-safe dish, and brush
them with oil.*

1. Wipe all the mushrooms,
only wash them if necessary.
Slice thinly and arrange in a
microwave-safe dish, together with the chopped shallots
and garlic clove. Moisten
with 4 tablespoons of the oil
and season with salt, pepper,
and thyme. Cover and cook
on *full power for 6–8 minutes*, stirring from time to
time.
2. Remove the mushrooms
from the oven, sprinkle with
the two types of vinegar, and
season to taste. Leave to
cool.
3. Meanwhile, sprinkle the
rabbit fillets with salt and
pepper. Arrange them on a
microwave-safe dish and
brush with oil. Cook uncovered on *full power for 2–3
minutes*. Turn the fillets over
halfway through the cooking
time. Cover with aluminum
foil and leave to cool.
4. Slice the rabbit fillets thinly and arrange on four plates

alongside the mushroom
salad.
Serving suggestion: serve
with whole-wheat bread rolls.
Recommended drink:
chilled beer or cider.

> ### TIP
> *Any combination
> of wild, fresh, or
> dried mushrooms
> will work equally
> well.*

BRAISED CALF'S SWEETBREADS WITH SALAD GREENS

SERVES 4 ◼◼

*For standard microwave
ovens (600 watts)
Preparation and cooking
time: 30 minutes
Soaking time: 2 hours
Kcal per portion: 155
P = 10g, F = 12g, C = 1g*

7 ounces calf's sweetbreads
1 cup veal or beef broth
1 tbsp white wine vinegar
½ bayleaf
5 peppercorns

FOR THE SALAD:
2 cups mixed salad greens,
such as lollo rosso, lettuce,
and radicchio

FOR THE VINAIGRETTE:
salt
1 tsp hot mustard
1 tsp raspberry vinegar
1 tsp wine vinegar
freshly ground black pepper
3 tbsps corn oil
1 tbsp nut oil

IN ADDITION:
4 sprigs chervil
4 cherry tomatoes

1. Soak the calf's sweetbreads for about 2 hours in
cold water. Change the
water 3 times. Remove any
membrane or fatty tissue.
2. Place the veal broth, vinegar, bayleaf, and pepper-
corns in a microwave dish
and cook at *full power for
4–5 minutes*. Add the sweetbreads, cover, and cook at
*full power for a further 2–4
minutes*, depending on the
thickness of the sweet-
breads. Turn them over
once. Leave the sweet-
breads to stand in the broth
for a few minutes.
3. Trim the salad greens,
wash thoroughly, and dry in
a salad spinner.
4. To make the vinaigrette,
combine the salt, mustard,

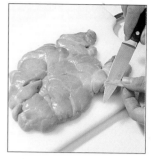

*Soak the sweetbreads for at least
2 hours, then remove any
membranes and fatty tissue.*

both types of vinegar, and
the pepper. Whisk until the
salt has dissolved. Add the
oil a few drops at a time, stirring constantly until the liquid thickens.
5. Toss the lettuce leaves in
the vinaigrette and arrange
them on four plates. Cut the
sweetbreads into slices and
arrange them on the leaves.
Garnish with chervil leaves
and quartered cherry tomatoes.
Recommended drink: white
wine, such as Moselle.

> ### TIP
> *Sweetbread is the
> culinary term for
> the thymus
> gland, the organ
> which controls
> growth. It
> contracts with
> age, so the best
> sweetbreads are
> from young
> animals. Round
> sweetbreads are
> found near the
> heart, while the
> longer, flatter
> ones are situated
> in the neck
> region.*

BEETROOT SALAD WITH HERB VINAIGRETTE

(photograph page 96/97)

SERVES 4 ■

*For standard microwave
   ovens (600 watts)
Preparation and cooking
   time: 30 minutes
Resting time: 2 hours
Kcal per portion: 145
P = 2g, F = 10g, C = 9g*

*8 medium raw beets
½ cup veal broth*

FOR THE VINAIGRETTE:

*1 tbsp red wine vinegar
3 tbsps red wine
salt
½ tsp Dijon mustard
4 tbsps olive oil
1 tbsp chopped shallots
1 tbsp fresh minced herbs
   (parsley, chervil, chives,
   basil)*

IN ADDITION:

*a few salad greens, such as
   Boston lettuce*

1. Wash the beets thoroughly. Peel and cut into ½-inch cubes. Add to the veal broth and place in a microwave-safe bowl, season with salt, cover, and cook at *full power for 13–15 minutes.* Leave to cool.
2. Combine the vinegar, red wine, salt, and mustard. Add the oil a few drops at a time, whisking constantly. Add the shallots and herbs to the vinaigrette and then mix with the cooked beets.
3. Chill the beets for at least 2 hours and serve with the salad greens.

ITALIAN POTATO SALAD

SERVES 4–6 ■■

*For standard microwave
   ovens (600 watts)
Preparation and cooking
   time: 45 minutes
Kcal per portion if serving 4:
   280
P = 5g, F = 16g, C = 28g*

*4 cups waxy potatoes
1 yellow bell pepper
1 red bell pepper
4 small onions
2 small zucchini
2 ripe beefsteak tomatoes
1–2 garlic cloves, chopped
sprig of thyme
sprig of rosemary
salt
freshly ground black pepper
6 tbsps dry white wine
6 tbsps olive oil
juice of 1 lemon
½ bunch parsley*

1. Wash and peel the potatoes. Cut into 1-inch cubes. Halve the peppers and remove the stalks and seeds. Wash well and cut into squares the same size as the potatoes. Peel and quarter the onions. Trim the zucchini and cut into ¼-inch slices.

TIP

This salad tastes best if served warm. In summer it is ideal with broiled and barbecued dishes, as it can be prepared in advance. If necessary, re-heat it in the microwave oven just before serving.

Add the olive oil and wine to the potatoes, peppers, garlic, and herbs.

Add the tomatoes and zucchini for the last 10 minutes.

2. Make two cuts across the top of the tomatoes and microwave at *full power for 2–4 minutes.*
3. Place the potatoes, peppers, and onions in a shallow, microwave-safe dish. Mix in the garlic and herbs and season with salt and pepper. Pour the olive oil and wine over the mixture and cook at *full power for 25–30 minutes,* stirring occasionally.
4. Peel and halve the beefsteak tomatoes. Remove the stalks and seeds and cut into 1-inch cubes. After 20 minutes of cooking time, mix the zucchini and tomatoes with the vegetables.
5. Sprinkle the cooked vegetables with lemon juice and season to taste. Add the chopped parsley and leave to stand for a few minutes before serving.
Recommended drink: a light, Italian red wine, such as Bardolino.

TURKISH EGGPLANT PURÉE

SERVES 4 ■

*For standard microwave
   ovens (600 watts)
Preparation and cooking
   time: 30 minutes
Kcal per portion: 150
P = 2g, F = 13g, C = 5g*

*1 eggplant
1–2 garlic cloves
1 small onion
3–4 tbsps olive oil
salt
freshly ground black pepper
pinch of sugar
2 tbsps lemon juice
1 tbsp yogurt
a few black olives
1 tbsp chopped parsley*

1. Trim, wash and dry the eggplant. Pierce with a fork all over, place on a plate, and cook on *full power for 8–10 minutes.* Turn over after 4–5 minutes.
2. Halve the eggplant and scoop out the flesh. Peel the garlic and onion and grind them in a food processor. Mix with the eggplant and purée again. Add the oil a few drops at a time. Season well with salt, pepper, sugar, and lemon juice and then stir in the yogurt.
3. Spoon the purée into a shallow bowl, smooth the surface, and garnish with olive halves and parsley.
Serving suggestion: fresh white bread.
Recommended drink: raki or ouzo (aniseed-flavoured spirit) with water.

CAULIFLOWER PÂTÉ WITH PRAWNS

SERVES 4–6 ■■

For standard microwave ovens (600 watts)
Preparation and cooking time: 30 minutes
Kcal per portion if serving 4: 210
P = 13g, F = 12g, C = 11g

1 small cauliflower
2 tbsps butter or margarine
2 tbsps all-purpose flour
1 cup milk
salt
freshly ground white pepper
freshly grated nutmeg
2 egg yolks
2 egg whites
½ cup frozen shrimp
fat for greasing

1. Trim the cauliflower and break it up into flowerets. Wash thoroughly. Purée half the cauliflower in a food processor and cut the rest into smaller flowerets.
2. Melt the butter or margarine in the microwave oven set to full power for 1 minute. Add the flour, stir well and cook on *full power for 1 minute.* Add the milk, whisking well and cook on *full power for 4–5 minutes,* stirring every 2 minutes.
3. Season this béchamel sauce with salt, pepper, and nutmeg. Leave to cool.
4. Stir in the puréed cauliflower flowerets and egg yolks. Whisk the egg whites until stiff and add the shrimp. Grease a microwave-safe 10-inch cake pan and cook on *full power for 5 minutes* and *medium power for 12–15 minutes.* Allow to cool, cut into slices, and serve with a plain green salad.

ZUCCHINI RING WITH CHOPPED TOMATOES

SERVES 4 ■

For standard microwave ovens (600 watts)
Preparation and cooking time: 30 minutes
Resting time: 30 minutes
Kcal per portion: 165
P = 6g, F = 11g, C = 10g

14 ounces zucchini
1 garlic clove
1 shallot
2 eggs
2 tbsps sour cream
salt
freshly ground white pepper
½ tsp hot mustard
fat for greasing
2 beefsteak tomatoes
1 tbsp chopped shallots
1 tsp balsamic vinegar
2 tbsps extra-virgin olive oil

1. Wash, trim, and slice the zucchini. Peel and chop the garlic and shallot and purée in a blender with the zucchini. Add the sour cream and eggs. Season with salt, pepper, and mustard.

> **TIP**
>
> *If a ring mold is not available, use a round, microwave-safe dish and place a ramekin or glass in the middle.*

2. Grease an 8-inch microwave-safe ring mold and spoon in the purée. Cover with microwave-safe plastic wrap and cook on *full power for 5 minutes* and *medium power* for *8–10 minutes.*
3. Meanwhile wash and halve the tomatoes. Discard the stalks and seeds and cut the flesh into cubes. Combine with the chopped shallots.

Add the eggs to the puréed zucchini.

Cover the ring mold with microwave-safe plastic wrap.

Marinate the chopped tomatoes and shallots in an oil-and-vinegar dressing.

4. Combine the salt and vinegar, add the oil, and pour this over the tomatoes. Leave to marinate.
5. Leave the zucchini ring to cool. Invert and place the marinated tomatoes in the middle.
Serving suggestion: wholewheat bread.
Recommended drink: a dry sherry (fino).

FARMHOUSE PÂTÉ

SERVES 8–10 ■■

For standard microwave ovens (600 watts)
Preparation and cooking time: 45 minutes
Resting time: several hours
Kcal per portion if serving 8: 435
P = 15g, F = 37g, C = 1g

1 onion
2 slices smoked, Canadian bacon
2 tbsps butter
8 ounces chicken livers
8 ounces pig's liver
8 ounces pork belly
2 eggs
3 tbsps kirsch
1 tbsp marjoram leaves
2 tbsps minced parsley
salt
freshly ground black pepper
fat for greasing

1. Chop the onion and smoked bacon. Place in a microwave-safe dish and cook on full power for 3–4 minutes.
2. Remove any membrane and fatty tissue from the chicken livers, add to the onions and bacon, and cook on full power for 2 minutes, stirring once.
3. Cut the pig's liver and pork belly into small pieces. Mix with the chicken livers and eggs and blend to a purée in a food processor. Season with the kirsch, herbs, and spices.
4. Spoon the mixture into a microwave-safe 8-inch terrine. Tap the terrine against the worktop once or twice to ensure all the air has escaped. Cover and cook on *full power for 10 minutes.*
5. Place a heavy weight over the pâté and leave overnight. Serve sliced.
Serving suggestion: serve with a cress salad.
Recommended drink: lite beer.

SAVOY CABBAGE ROLLS STUFFED WITH MUSHROOMS

SERVES 4 ■ ■ ■

*For standard microwave
   ovens (600 watts)
Preparation and cooking
   time: 40 minutes
Kcal per portion: 250
P = 10g, F = 22g, C = 2g*

4 large Savoy cabbage leaves
2 cups mixed fresh wild
   mushrooms
2 tbsps chopped shallots
2 tbsps butter or margarine
1 cup cream cheese
2 tbsps chopped parsley
3 tbsps grated Swiss cheese
salt
freshly ground black pepper
4 tbsps beef or veal broth
2 tbsps sour cream

1. Wash the Savoy cabbage leaves, wrap in a cloth while still wet, and cook at full power for 3–4 minutes.
2. Wipe the mushrooms but only wash them if really necessary. Cut them into slices. Place the chopped shallots in a microwave-safe dish and cook at *full power for 2 minutes.*
3. Add the mushrooms and butter or margarine. Cover and cook at *full power for 4–5 minutes.*
4. Stir together the cream cheese, parsley, and 2 tablespoons Swiss cheese. Add the cooled mushrooms, season with salt and pepper, and leave to cool.
5. Spread the cabbage leaves out flat and coat each one with a layer of the mushroom-and-cream mixture. Fold in the sides and roll up. Arrange the rolls side-by-side in a microwave-safe dish and pour the veal broth over them. Combine the sour cream and the remaining cream cheese and spread a little on each of the Savoy cabbage rolls.

Wrap the wet Savoy cabbage leaves in a cloth and microwave them.

Spread mushroom filling onto the leaves and roll up.

Pour a little veal broth over the rolls before topping with cheese.

6. Cover and cook at *full power for 3–4 minutes.* Uncover and cook at *full power for a further 2 minutes.*
7. If using a combination oven, sprinkle a tablespoon of cheese over the rolls and brown under the broiler. Add a little minced parsley, if required.
Recommended drink: a white wine.

STUFFED TOMATOES WITH CHEESE AU GRATIN

SERVES 4 ■

*For combination microwave
   ovens (600 watts)
Preparation and cooking
   time: 20 minutes
Kcal per portion: 160
P = 8g, F = 12g, C = 4g*

4 large ripe tomatoes
salt
freshly ground black pepper
2 anchovies in oil
8 black olives
½ tsp dried thyme
3 eggs
2 tbsps heavy cream
3 tbsps grated Swiss or Jack
   cheese

1. Wash the tomatoes. Cut a "lid" off each tomato and remove the seeds and inner pulp. Sprinkle salt and pepper inside and chop the lid into cubes.
2. Cut the anchovies into short lengths. Pit and quarter the olives, and mix with the thyme leaves.
3. Beat together the cream and eggs. Add the chopped tomatoes, anchovies, olives, thyme, and 1 tbsp of cheese.
4. Switch on the broiler of the combination oven.
5. Place the hollowed tomatoes on a microwave-safe dish and fill with the mixture.
6. Sprinkle the remaining cheese on top of the mixture and broil at full power for 2–3 minutes.
Recommended drink: a light red wine, e.g. from Provence.

CROSTINI WITH CHICKEN LIVERS

SERVES 4–6 ■ ■

*For standard microwave
   ovens (600 watts)
Preparation and cooking
   time: 30 minutes
Kcal per portion if serving 4:
   360
P = 24g, F = 10g, C = 39g*

1 small onion
2 tbsps olive oil
1½ cups chicken livers
sprig of thyme
2 tbsps tomato juice
6 tbsps chicken broth
salt
freshly ground black pepper
2 anchovies
1 tbsp capers
1 tbsp chopped herbs
6 large slices Italian
   flatbread (foccacia)
fresh thyme leaves to garnish

1. Peel and chop the onion. Place in a microwave-safe dish with the olive oil and cook at *full power for 2–3 minutes.*
2. Remove any skin and fatty tissues from the chicken livers and chop into small pieces. Add them to the onions and cook, uncovered, at *full power for 3–4 minutes.*
3. Add the thyme, tomato liquid, and broth. Season with salt and pepper and cook at *full power for 4–5 minutes.* Strain the mixture through a sieve.
4. Chop the anchovies finely and mix with chicken liver purée, together with the capers and herbs.
5. Toast the bread and spread it with the mixture, either warm or cold. Sprinkle with thyme leaves and cut the toasted slices into fingers.
Recommended   drink: Italian white wine.

105

PUFF PASTRY ROLLS STUFFED WITH EXOTIC VEGETABLES

SERVES 4 ■ ■ ■
*For combination microwave
ovens (600 watts)
Preparation and cooking
time: 1 hour
Soaking time: 2 hours
Kcal per portion: 465
P = 7g, F = 35g, C = 24g*

1 tsp dried Chinese
   mushrooms (cloud-ears)
10 ounces frozen puff dough
1 thin leek
¼ head Chinese cabbage
3 tbsps oil
½ cup soy beansprouts
bunch of parsley, minced
3 tbsps soy sauce
4 tbsps dry sherry (fino)
freshly ground black pepper
generous pinch dried
   lemongrass or grated rind
   of 1 lemon
½ tsp Chinese five-spice
   powder
1 tsp chopped ginger
1 egg yolk for the glaze

1. Soak the dried mushrooms in lukewarm water for
about 2 hours. Thaw the
frozen puff dough.

TIP

*Serve with soy
sauce or hoisin
sauce.*

---

2. Trim the leek, wash, and
slice thinly. Cut the Chinese
cabbage into strips. Place
both in a microwave-safe
dish with the oil. Cook
uncovered at *full power for
4–5 minutes,* stirring from
time to time.
3. Add the beansprouts,
drained mushrooms, and the
minced parsley. Season with
soy sauce, sherry, and the
herbs and spices. Cook at
*full power for a further 4–5
minutes.*

*Cut the puff pastry sheet into
rectangles about 4 x 5 inches.*

*Place a spoonful of the vegetable
filling in the center of each
rectangle. Fold over the pastry
and press the edges together with
the prongs of a fork or a pastry
crimper.*

4. Place the thawed puff
dough on top of each other
and roll out to a thickness of
about ⅛ inch. Cut into rectangles about 4 x 5 inches.
5. Heat the oven to 450°F.
6. Spoon a little of the mixture onto each rectangle of
dough and brush a little
water around the edges.
Fold over to make rolls and
place on a baking sheet
lined with nonstick baking
paper. Brush the surfaces
with a little egg yolk and
bake at *450°F (fan-assisted
400°F) for 10 minutes* or until
golden-brown.
Recommended drink: a dry
sherry (fino.)

SAUSAGE PARCELS

SERVES 6–8 ■ ■
*For combination microwave
ovens (600 watts)
Preparation and cooking
time: 40 minutes
Kcal per portion if serving 6:
470
P = 12g, F = 34g, C = 25g*

FOR THE DOUGH:
2 cups all-purpose flour
salt
freshly grated nutmeg
½ cup butter
4–6 tbsps milk

FOR THE FILLING:
10 ounces sausagemeat
1 egg yolk
1 tsp marjoram leaves

FOR THE GLAZE:
1 egg yolk
1 tbsp cream

1. Place the flour, salt, and nutmeg in a bowl. Cut the butter
into dice and mix with the
flour. Add the milk and knead
to a smooth dough.
2. Knead the dough again on
a floured worktop. Roll out
the dough into a rectangle
and cut into 5-inch squares.
3. Add the egg yolk and marjoram to the sausagemeat.
4. Heat the oven to 450°F.
5. Spoon a little filling onto
each square, brush water
around the edges, and fold
over to make rolls. Place the
rolls, seam side downward,
on a baking sheet lined with
nonstick baking paper. Cut
the remaining pieces of pastry into bows and thin ribbons
and use to decorate the top of
the parcels. Beat the egg yolk
and cream and brush over the
parcels to glaze.
6. Bake on the lower shelf of
the oven at *450°F (fan-assisted 400°F) for 10–12 minutes*
or until golden-brown.
Recommended drink: beer.

WARM LEEK SALAD WITH LEMON SAUCE

SERVES 4 ■
*For standard microwave
ovens (600 watts)
Preparation and cooking
time: 25 minutes
Kcal per portion: 185
P = 5g, F = 17g, C = 3g*

4 small leeks
½ cup veal broth
salt

FOR THE VINAIGRETTE:
2 tbsps lemon juice
salt
1 tsp shallot mustard
white pepper
5 tbsps neutral oil

IN ADDITION:
4 slices smoked tongue
1 tbsp chopped parsley

1. Trim the leeks and discard
the green leaves. Cut the
white flesh diagonally into ¼-
inch slices. Rinse thoroughly
and drain in a colander.
2. Place the leek rings in a
microwave-safe dish and
arrange the leek slices on
top of each other but no
deeper than 1 inch. Pour
over the veal broth, season
with salt, cover and cook at
full power for 6–8 minutes.
Leave to stand for a few minutes.
3. To make the vinaigrette,
whisk together the lemon
juice, salt, mustard, salt and
pepper until the salt has dissolved. Continue to whisk,
while adding the oil.
4. Pour the lemon vinaigrette over the leeks and
arrange on a dish. Cut the
smoked tongue into thin
slices and arrange them over
the leek salad, together with
the parsley. Serve warm.
Serving suggestion: serve
with home-baked bread.
Recommended drink: Pils or
lager.

Lean Cuisine

The message that this chapter gives to those who need to keep an eye on their weight is simple, namely, that you can go easy on the calories without spoiling the natural flavors. Not surprisingly, raw ingredients play an important part in meeting slimmers' daily nutritional requirements, so fresh vegetables, fruit, and tasty herbs are very much in evidence. Less desirable are those richer, fatty foods such as sour cream, oil, and butter, but there's no need to stint on cucumber, tomatoes, fennel and, of course, herbs.

If you prefer to leave raw vegetables out of your repertoire of starters, then branch out into new culinary fields. Try Steamed Chicken Dumplings or Fried Tofu with Sweet-and-sour Vegetables. If you have a guest who is slimming and wants to forego appetizers altogether as one way of avoiding temptation, then make the salad portions a little more generous and serve salad as an entrée.

Artichoke Hearts in Tomato Vinaigrette (recipe page 120)

APPLE SALAD WITH MUNG BEANSPROUTS

SERVES 4 ■
*Preparation and cooking
    time: 30 minutes
Kcal per portion: 130
P = 2g, F = 6g, C = 17g*

*500g/1lb 2oz tart apples,
    preferably red
100g/4oz mung bean sprouts
1 punnet cress*

FOR THE DRESSING:
*1 tsp honey
1 tsp soy sauce
½ tsp grated horseradish
salt
1 tbsp cider vinegar
2 tbsps sunflower oil
freshly ground black pepper*

1. Wash and quarter the apples. Remove the core, but do not peel. Slice each segment thinly and mix with the mung beansprouts and snipped cress.

> **TIP**
>
> *Mung
> beansprouts can
> be bought in
> health food stores
> and
> supermarkets but
> they can also be
> sprouted at
> home.*

2. To make the dressing, combine the honey, soy sauce, horseradish, salt, and vinegar. Add the oil a little at a time, whisking constantly. Season well with pepper and pour this over the salad.

MÂCHE WITH PINK GRAPEFRUIT AND TOASTED SUNFLOWER SEEDS

SERVES 4 ■
*Preparation and cooking
    time: 30 minutes
Kcal per portion: 150
P = 4g, F = 9g, C = 13g*

*7 ounces mâche
2 pink grapefruit
2 tbsps shelled sunflower
    seeds*

FOR THE DRESSING:
*1 tsp maple syrup
salt
1 tsp balsamic vinegar
1 tbsp walnut oil
1 tbsp sunflower oil
freshly ground black pepper
pinch of cayenne pepper*

1. Snip off the root ends of the mâche but leave each plant intact. Wash thoroughly, in several rinses, as grains of grit and sand need to be rinsed out. Spin dry in a salad spinner.
2. Peel the grapefruit thickly so that the white parts are removed. Carefully remove the segments from their skins using a sharp knife. Reserve the grapefruit juice. Mix with the mâche in a shallow bowl.
3. Toast the sunflower seeds in a skillet.
4. To make the dressing, mix the maple syrup with the grapefruit juice. Add salt and vinegar and whisk well until all the salt has dissolved. Add the oils a few drops at a time, whisking constantly. Season with pepper and cayenne pepper.
5. Toss the lettuce and grapefruit segments in the dressing and serve with the toasted sunflower seeds.

*Wash the lamb's lettuce
thoroughly and then spin dry.*

*Peel the grapefruit and remove
the white parts.*

*Use a sharp knife to remove the
grapefruit segments from their
skins.*

RED, WHITE AND GREEN SALAD

SERVES 4 ■
*Preparation and cooking
    time: 20 minutes
Kcal per portion: 40
P = 1g, F = 3g, C = 3g*

*1 young white radish
    (daikon)
bunch of small radishes
1 small cucumber*

FOR THE DRESSING:
*salt
2 tbsps white wine vinegar
1 tbsp sunflower oil
freshly ground white pepper
bunch of chives, finely
    chopped*

1. Trim the white radish and small radishes and wash thoroughly with the cucumber. Peel the white radish.
2. Trim the narrow ends of the cucumber. Slice the cucumber and both types of radish thinly, using a slicer or sharp knife and place in a bowl.
3. To make the dressing, whisk together the salt and vinegar until the salt has dissolved. Add the oil, stirring constantly, and then pour the dressing over the salad ingredients. Sprinkle with pepper and finely chopped chives and mix together.

> **TIP**
>
> *A refreshing
> salad to eat with
> broiled and
> barbecued meats
> or else by itself
> with whole-wheat
> bread and butter.*

FENNEL WITH MANGO

SERVES 4 ■

*Preparation and cooking
    time: 20 minutes
Kcal per portion: 120
P = 4g, F = 3g, C = 17g*

*2 small fennel bulbs
1 small ripe mango
1 orange*

FOR THE DRESSING:

*1 tbsp sour cream substitute
2 tbsps low-fat yogurt
1 tbsp lemon juice
2 tbsps orange juice
salt
pinch of cayenne pepper
1 tbsp shelled toasted
    pumpkin seeds (pepitas)
for the garnish*

1. Wash the fennel bulbs, cut off the leaves, and chop finely. Halve the bulbs and cut each half into thin strips.
2. Peel the mango and cut the flesh from the stone in wedges, and then dice. Peel the orange and scrape off the white parts. Remove the segments from their skin and mix with the fennel strips and diced mango.
3. Stir together the sour cream, yogurt, orange and lemon juice, salt, and cayenne pepper to make a smooth sauce. Add the chopped fennel leaves to the salad ingredients and toss in the dressing. Finally add the pumpkin seeds.

> **TIP**
>
> *Try pinenuts
> instead of
> pumpkin seeds.*

*Cut off the fennel leaves and
chop finely.*

*Halve the fennel bulbs and slice
thinly.*

*Peel the mango with a sharp
knife.*

*Cut the flesh from the stone in
wedges.*

TROPICAL ENDIVE SALAD

SERVES 4 ■■

*Preparation and cooking
    time: 30 minutes
Kcal per portion: 150
P = 3g, F = 4g, C = 24g*

*2 large endive heads
1 orange
1 kiwi fruit
1 small banana
½ ripe mango
4 fresh dates*

FOR THE DRESSING:

*2 tbsps low-fat mayonnaise
½ cup low-fat yogurt
1 tsp mild curry powder
dash of Tabasco sauce
juice of 1 lemon
generous pinch of ground
    lemongrass or grated rind
    of ½ lemon
½ tsp chopped chili pepper*

1. Wash and halve the endive. Trim off the stalks and cut into strips. Peel the orange and scrape off the white parts. Remove the orange segments from their skins. Peel and slice the kiwi fruit and banana. Remove the mango flesh and dice it. Slit open the skin of the dates with a sharp knife. Halve each date, pit it, and halve again. Place all the prepared ingredients in a bowl.
2. To make the dressing, stir together the mayonnaise, yogurt, and curry powder and season with the Tabasco sauce, lemon juice, and lemongrass or grated lemon rind. Pour the dressing over the salad ingredients and toss. Garnish with the chopped chili pepper.

BROCCOLI SALAD WITH SHRIMP

SERVES 4 ■■

*Preparation and cooking
    time: 40 minutes
Kcal per portion: 80
P = 9g, F = 3g, C = 4g*

*1¼ pounds broccoli
salt
½ cup shelled shrimp
juice of ½ lemon*

FOR THE DRESSING:

*2 tbsps sour cream substitute
½ cup low-fat yogurt
2 tbsps lemon juice
salt
generous pinch of cayenne
    pepper
grated rind of ½ lemon
1 tbsp chopped chives*

1. Wash the broccoli and remove any leaves. Cut the thick stalk into pieces and break off the flowerets. Bring a little salted water to the boil in a medium saucepan and cook the broccoli for 12–15 minutes until firm.
2. Place the shrimp in a bowl, add the lemon juice, cover, and chill in the refrigerator.
3. Drain the broccoli in a colander, plunge immediately into ice-cold water, and leave to drain.
4. To make the dressing, mix together the sour cream substitute and low-fat yogurt. Season with lemon juice, salt, cayenne pepper, and lemon rind. Finally, add the chopped chives.
5. Arrange the broccoli on a dish, pour the dressing over it and garnish with shrimp.

LEAN
CUISINE

MULTI-COLORED POTATO SALAD

SERVES 4　■
Preparation and cooking
*   time: 30 minutes*
Resting time: 1 hour
Kcal per portion: 150
P = 3g, F = 6g, C = 22g

2 cups waxy potatoes
½ cucumber
2 tomatoes
1 small apple
2 green onions (scallions)
½ bunch rocket or watercress

FOR THE DRESSING:
salt
2 tbsps white wine vinegar
5 tbsps hot water or broth
2 tbsps oil
freshly ground black pepper
2 tbsps chopped chives

1. Wash the potatoes and
boil in their jackets until
cooked. Drain and cool.

*Chop all the vegetables on a
chopping board.*

┌─────────────┐
│　　**TIP**　　│
│ *For a satisfying* │
│ *meal, add some* │
│ *sliced low-fat* │
│ *wieners or franks* │
│ *to this salad.* │
└─────────────┘

*Peel the cooked potatoes, dice
and mix with the other salad
ingredients.*

2. While the potatoes are
cooking, wash the cucum-
ber and dice it, but do not
peel it. Wash the tomatoes
and cut them into segments.
Peel and halve the apple.
Remove the core and dice.
Cut the green onions (scallions) into rings and cut the
rocket or watercress into
strips.
3. When the potatoes have
cooled, peel them. Dice
them and mix with the other
ingredients in the bowl.
4. To make the dressing,
combine the salt, vinegar,
water or broth, oil, and pepper. Toss the salad ingredients and chopped chives in
the dressing. Leave to stand
for about an hour.

ZUCCHINI AND CARROTS WITH AN ORANGE VINAIGRETTE

SERVES 4　■
Preparation and cooking
*   time: 20 minutes*
Kcal per portion: 105
P = 2g, F = 6g, C = 11g

3 small zucchini
3 young carrots
1 orange

FOR THE VINAIGRETTE:
salt
1 tsp Dijon mustard
1 tsp honey
3 tbsps freshly squeezed
*   orange juice*
1 tbsp freshly squeezed lemon
*   juice*
2 tbsps extra virgin olive oil
freshly ground black pepper

FOR THE GARNISH:
grated orange rind
5–6 chopped basil leaves

1. Wash and trim the zucchini. Wash the carrots and
scrape if necessary. Slice
both vegetables lengthwise
and then across into thin
strips.

┌─────────────┐
│　　**TIP**　　│
│ *Use only young,* │
│ *fresh zucchini* │
│ *and carrots.* │
└─────────────┘

2. Peel the orange and discard the white parts. Remove
the orange segments from
their skins. Cut the segments
into smaller pieces and add
to the vegetables.
3. To make the vinaigrette,
combine the salt, honey, and
mustard. Gradually add the
orange and lemon juice and
the oil. Season with pepper
and whisk until the sauce
becomes creamy.
4. Pour the orange dressing
over the salad ingredients,
stir well, and sprinkle with
the freshly-grated orange
rind and the chopped basil
leaves.

*Wash and trim the carrots and
zucchini and cut them into thin
strips.*

*Use a zester to cut wafer-thin
slices of orange rind.*

*Whisk the vinaigrette with a
balloon whisk.*

114

SUMMER SALAD
WITH SHRIMP AND CUCUMBER

SUMMER SALAD WITH SHRIMP AND CUCUMBER

SERVES 4 ■
*Preparation and cooking
time: 15 minutes
Kcal per portion: 100
P = 8g, F = 6g, C = 3g*

*1 cucumber
⅔ cup shelled shrimp*

FOR THE VINAIGRETTE:
*1 tbsp white wine vinegar
1 tbsp lemon juice
salt
2 tbsps oil
freshly ground black pepper*

IN ADDITION:
bunch of dill, chopped

1. Peel the cucumber and trim off the ends. Cut into thin slices with a vegetable slicer. Place in a bowl with the shrimp.

TIP

*The best
cucumbers are
undoubtedly
those grown
outdoors. On hot
summer days,
this salad can
make a light,
refreshing meal
for two people or
an appetizer for
four.*

2. To make the vinaigrette, combine the vinegar, lemon juice, and salt, stirring until the salt has dissolved. Add the oil a little at a time, stirring constantly, and season with pepper. Toss the salad ingredients in the vinaigrette. Add the chopped dill and leave the salad to stand for a few minutes.

RADICCHIO AND ROCKET SALAD WITH PARMESAN

SERVES 4 ■
*Preparation and cooking
time: 15 minutes
Kcal per portion: 100
P = 5g, F = 8g, C = 1g*

*bunch of rocket
small head of radicchio
lettuce*

FOR THE VINAIGRETTE:
*salt
1 tbsp red wine vinegar
1 tsp balsamic vinegar
generous pinch mustard
powder
freshly-ground black pepper
1 tbsp olive oil
1 tbsp walnut oil*

IN ADDITION:
*2-ounce piece mild
Parmesan cheese*

1. Pick over the rocket leaves and cut off the thicker stalks. Cut out the core from the radicchio and remove the leaves. Tear the radicchio and rocket leaves into smaller pieces. Wash thoroughly and spin-dry in a salad spinner.

TIP

*Rocket plant is a
native of the
Mediterranean
region. It is now
much in demand
as a leaf salad
and is cultivated
widely, especially
in California.*

2. To make the vinaigrette, combine the salt, the two types of vinegar, mustard and pepper, stirring until the salt has completely dissolved. Add the oils a few drops at a time, whisking constantly.

3. Toss the salad ingredients in the vinaigrette and then arrange the leaves on four plates. Crumble the Parmesan cheese over the top.

Separate the lettuce leaves and tear them into small pieces.

Wash thoroughly and dry in a salad spinner.

Crumble the Parmesan cheese with a fork.

SAUERKRAUT SALAD WITH GRAPES

SERVES 4 ■
*Preparation and cooking
time: 20 minutes
Resting time: 30 minutes
Kcal per portion: 175
P = 2g, F = 10g, C = 16g*

*1½ cups sauerkraut, rinsed
and drained
1 red apple
7 ounces black grapes*

FOR THE DRESSING:
*salt
1–2 tbsps white wine vinegar
1 tbsp maple syrup
4 tbsps white wine
2 tbsps oil
freshly ground black pepper*

1. Chop the sauerkraut. Quarter and core the apple and cut across the segments to make thin slices.
Wash and halve the grapes. If necessary, remove the seeds. Mix together all the ingredients in a bowl.
2. To make the dressing, combine the salt, vinegar, maple syrup, and white wine. Add the oil a few drops at a time, stirring constantly. Season with pepper and toss the salad in the dressing. Leave to stand for at least 30 minutes.

TIP

*Sauerkraut is a
good source of
fiber, is also rich
in vitamin C, and
contains just 25
Kcal per 100g.*

SNOW PEA SALAD WITH CHERRY TOMATOES

SERVES 4 ■

Preparation and cooking time: 20 minutes
Resting time: 30 minutes
Kcal per portion: 315
P = 18g, F = 6g, C = 44g

1½ cups snow peas
salt

FOR THE VINAIGRETTE:
2 tbsps white wine vinegar
salt
½ tsp Dijon mustard
2 tbsps oil
1 tbsp chopped shallots
1 tbsp mixed spring herbs
freshly ground black pepper

IN ADDITION:
1 cup cherry tomatoes

---

1. Top and tail the snow peas and, if necessary, remove any stringy fibers. Bring plenty of salted water to the boil and blanch the snow peas for 3–5 minutes. Strain in a colander and then dip in ice-cold water for a few moments. Leave to drain.
2. To make the vinaigrette, combine the vinegar, salt, and mustard, stirring until the salt has dissolved. Add the oil, stirring constantly. Finally, add the chopped shallots, herbs, and pepper.
3. Place the snow peas in a bowl and toss them in the vinaigrette. Leave to stand for about 30 minutes.
4. Wash and quarter the cherry tomatoes and mix with the salad ingredients.
5. Serve the salad in four small bowls.

JAPANESE-STYLE MUSSEL SALAD

SERVES 4 ■■

Preparation and cooking time: 30 minutes
Resting time: 15 minutes
Kcal per portion: 115
P = 6g, F = 3g, C = 5g

5 cups fresh mussels in their shells
½ cup sake (rice wine) or dry sherry (fino)
½ cup water
salt
1 small cucumber
2 green onions (scallions)
2 tomatoes

FOR THE DRESSING:
salt
2 tbsps rice vinegar or cider vinegar
2 tbsps sake or dry sherry (fino)
1 tbsp miso (soy bean paste)
¼ tsp wasabi or
½ tsp grated horseradish
1 tbsp sesame oil

---

1. Scrub the mussels thoroughly and discard any that have opened.

> **T I P**
>
> *Wasabi is Japanese horseradish and is available fresh, powdered or in a paste. In whatever form, it is very hot. Always use sparingly.*

2. Bring the rice wine and water to the boil in a large shallow saucepan. Add the mussels and a little salt. Cover and cook for 3–4 minutes over a gentle heat. Strain the opened mussels in a colander and leave to cool. Discard any which have not opened.
3. Wash the salad vegetables thoroughly. Slice the cucum-

Slice the cucumber and green onions thinly.

Remove the mussels from their shells.

Whisk together all the ingredients for the dressing.

ber. Chop the spring onions into rings, including some of the green parts. Slice the tomatoes into segments.
4. Remove the mussels from their shells and mix with the chopped vegetables.
5. To make the dressing, whisk together all the dressing ingredients and pour over the mussels and salad vegetables. Stir well and leave for about 15 minutes.

CHICKEN SALAD WITH SWEETCORN AND PEPPERS

SERVES 4 ■

Preparation and cooking time: 20 minutes
Resting time: 30 minutes
Kcal per portion: 600
P = 43g, F = 18g, C = 60g

1 cooked chicken
1 red pepper
1 green pepper
1 small onion
1 garlic clove
1 small can sweetcorn

FOR THE DRESSING:
salt
1 tbsp tomato ketchup
½ tsp chili pepper sauce
freshly ground black pepper
2 tbsps red wine vinegar
2 tbsps oil
1 tbsp minced parsley to garnish

---

1. Heat the oven to 475°F.
2. Skin the chicken, remove any bones and cut into cubes.
3. Wash the peppers. Place them on the middle shelf of the oven and bake until the skin splits (about 10–15 minutes). Turn the peppers over from time to time.
4. Peel and chop the garlic and onion. Peel the skin off the peppers, halve them, and remove the stalk and seeds. Cut the flesh into cubes and mix with the sweetcorn, onion, and garlic.
5. To make the dressing, whisk all the ingredients together. Toss the chicken and vegetables in the dressing and leave to stand for at least 30 minutes. Serve sprinkled with parsley.

CUCUMBER BOATS WITH VEGETABLE CHEESE

SERVES 2 ■■

*Preparation and cooking
time: 20 minutes
Kcal per portion: 190
P = 20g, F = 6g, C = 13g*

1 small cucumber
salt
freshly ground black pepper
1 cup low-fat soft cheese
2 tbsps light cream
1 small shallot
½ garlic clove
½ small red pepper
½ small green pepper
1 small carrot
bunch of cress
2 tsps tarragon mustard

1. Wash the cucumber and cut off strips of the peel to create a pattern of green and white strips. Halve it lengthwise, scoop out the seeds with a teaspoon, and sprinkle lightly with salt and pepper.
2. Blend the cheese and cream.

Slice off strips of cucumber peel.

Chop the carrot and garlic finely.

Spoon the mixture into a piping bag fitted with a wide nozzle.

> **TIP**
> *A chopped hard-cooked egg can be added to the mixture if liked.*

3. Peel and chop the garlic and shallot. Wash the peppers and cut into tiny squares. Peel and grate the carrot. Wash the cress. Chop half the cress and mix with the cheese and cream and the other vegetables. Season with the mustard, salt, and pepper.
4. Spoon the mixture into a piping bag fitted with a broad nozzle and pipe into the hollowed cucumber. Garnish with the remaining cress.

PEAR SALAD WITH SMOKED TROUT

SERVES 4 ■

*Preparation and cooking
time: 20 minutes
Kcal per portion: 110
P = 5g, F = 6g, C = 7g*

2 medium pears
4 ounces smoked trout fillets
2 sprigs fresh marjoram

FOR THE VINAIGRETTE:
salt
1–2 tbsps lemon juice
2 tbsps oil
freshly ground black pepper

1. Peel the pears and cut out the cores. Halve the pears lengthwise and then cut into thin wedges. Arrange them in layers on four plates.
2. Cut the trout fillets into small pieces and arrange alongside the pear wedges. Wash the marjoram leaves and sprinkle half of them over the pears and smoked trout fillets.
3. To make the vinaigrette, chop the remaining marjoram and mix in a bowl with the salt and lemon juice. Whisk constantly while adding the oil a few drops at a time. Continue until the vinaigrette develops a creamy consistency.
4. Pour the vinaigrette over the pears and sprinkle with pepper.

> **TIP**
> *For best results, choose only the ripest and juiciest pears.*

ARTICHOKE HEARTS IN TOMATO VINAIGRETTE

(photograph page 108/109)

SERVES 2 ■

*Preparation and cooking
time: 15 minutes
Kcal per portion: 70
P = 1g, F = 5g, C = 4g*

4 canned artichoke hearts
2 tomatoes

FOR THE VINAIGRETTE:
salt
generous pinch of Dijon
mustard
1 tbsp white wine vinegar
1 tbsp olive oil
1 tbsp chopped shallots
1 tsp chopped parsley
freshly ground black pepper
sprig of chervil

1. Remove the artichoke hearts from the jar or can, leave to drain and then halve. Arrange 4 halves in a circle in the middle of each plate.
2. Blanch the tomatoes. Peel, halve, and remove the seeds and stalk. Cut the flesh into cubes.

> **TIP**
> *Try making this starter with fresh baby artichokes. Boiled for just a few minutes, they taste really delicious.*

3. Stir together the salt, mustard, and vinegar until the salt dissolves. Continue stirring, while adding the oil. Add the chopped tomatoes and shallots, followed by the parsley.
4. Pour the vinaigrette over the artichoke hearts. Sprinkle with pepper and garnish with chervil.

**FRIED TOFU WITH
SWEET-AND-SOUR VEGETABLES**

FRIED TOFU WITH SWEET-AND-SOUR VEGETABLES

SERVES 2 ■■

*Preparation and cooking
time: 30 minutes*
Kcal per portion: about 455
P = 24g, F = 21g, C = 37g

4 green onions (scallions)
1 carrot
*½ cup fresh shiitake
   mushrooms or brown-
   capped mushrooms*
½ cup snow peas
1 cup tofu
3 tbsps sesame oil
salt
freshly ground black pepper
*generous pinch of ground
   ginger*
½ tsp Chinese five-spice
*2 tbsps rice wine or dry
   sherry (fino)*
1 tsp maple syrup
1 tbsp soy sauce

1. Trim and wash the vegetables. Slice the green onions into rings, chop the carrot, and slice the mushrooms thinly. Top and tail the snow peas and remove any stringy threads.
2. Cut the tofu into two equal portions. Heat 1 tablespoon of oil in a nonstick skillet and fry the tofu on both sides, allowing 1–2 minutes per side. Sprinkle with salt, pepper, ginger, and five-spice. Cover and keep warm.
3. Heat the remaining oil in a wok or a sauté pan and quickly fry the vegetables one after the other, stirring well. Season with salt, pepper, rice wine, or sherry, maple syrup, and soy sauce.
4. Cut the tofu into slices diagonally, arrange on warmed plates and cover with the fried vegetables.

STEAMED CHICKEN DUMPLINGS

SERVES 4 ■■■

*Preparation and cooking
time: 40 minutes*
Kcal per portion: 215
P = 15g, F = 8g, C = 19g

FOR THE DOUGH:
1 cup all-purpose flour
6–8 tbsps water
1 tsp oil

FOR THE FILLING:
6 ounces chicken breast
½ cup frozen leaf spinach
1 tbsp sesame oil
6 tbsps shrimp
*2 tbsps canned unsweetened
   coconut milk or 2 tbsps
   shredded coconut*
2 tbsps soy sauce
*½ tsp ground lemongrass or
   grated rind of 1 lemon*
salt
freshly ground black pepper
1 tbsp toasted sesame seeds
½ bunch chives

1. Combine the flour, water, and oil to make a smooth dough. Cover with a cloth and leave for 15 minutes.

> ## TIP
>
> *These dumplings
> can also be
> served in a soup.
> You could buy the
> dough ready
> made at a
> Chinese
> supermarket, or
> use wonton
> wrappers. The
> chicken could be
> replaced by
> shrimp.*

2. Meanwhile, cut the chicken flesh into small, thin slices. Chop the thawed spinach leaves coarsely.
3. Heat the oil in a wok or a sauté pan. Over high heat, stir-fry first the meat, then

*Cut out dough circles with a
cookie cutter and place a little
filling in the center.*

*Pull up the sides of the dough
around the filling to make little
dumplings.*

the shrimp, and finally the spinach. Add the coconut milk and soy sauce. Season with lemongrass or grated lemon rind, salt, and pepper. Continue to fry until all the liquid has evaporated. Add the sesame seeds and leave to cool.
4. On a floured worktop, roll out the dough as thinly as possible. Pull the dough sheets with your fingertips to make a wafer-thin sheet and cut out 12 circles about 4 inches in diameter. Place a little filling in the middle of each circle and pull up the sides to make little parcels. Twist the top and tie with a chive.
5. Place the dumpling in a bamboo basket or a sieve, cover, and steam above a little boiling water for a few minutes.
6. Arrange the dumplings on four plates and serve with soy sauce or hoisin sauce.

EGGS STUFFED WITH PRAWNS AND DILL

SERVES 4 ■■

*Preparation and cooking
time: 20 minutes*
Kcal per portion: 140
P = 12g, F = 8g, C = 2g

4 hard-boiled eggs
½ cup low-fat soft cheese
½ cup shelled shrimp
1 tsp lemon juice
*generous pinch of cayenne
   pepper*
salt
freshly ground black pepper
bunch of dill

FOR THE SALAD:
½ lettuce
salt
1 tsp white wine vinegar
1 tbsp oil

1. Shell and halve the hard-boiled eggs. Remove the yolk, place in a bowl, and crush with a fork. Gradually add the cream cheese, stirring well.
2. Chop the shrimp and mix with the egg-and-cheese mixture. Season well with lemon juice, cayenne pepper, salt and pepper.
3. Shape the egg-and-cheese mixture into balls the size of egg yolks. Wash the dill and chop finely. Dip the balls in the dill and return to the egg whites.
4. Wash the lettuce leaves, spin dry, and toss in a vinaigrette of salt, vinegar, and oil.
5. Arrange the salad on four plates and place two egg halves on top of each one.

Index